# PRELUDE TO PANIC

## The Story of the Bank Holiday

By Lawrence Sullivan

STATESMAN PRESS
Washington, D. C.

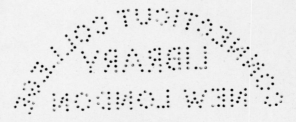
Printed in U.S.A.

"It is sheer presumption to attempt to remodel existing institutions without the least knowledge how they were formed, or whence they grew; to deal with social questions without a thought how society arose; to construct a social creed without an idea of fifty creeds that have risen and vanished before. Few men would, intentionally, attempt so much; but many do it unconsciously."

—FREDERIC HARRISON,
*The Meaning of History*
(New York, 1894)

# FOREWORD

World economic recovery began in the summer of 1932, but seven months later, in March, 1933, the United States experienced the most violent financial debacle in modern history.

How did it come about that our American house thus burst into flame anew, months after the world conflagration had been extinguished? What forces and circumstances turned the first gentle zephyrs of world restoration into the tornado of fear and panic which swept this nation, in forty dreadful days, to the very brink of chaos?

An extensive literature, already at hand, presents the events and policies which have prevailed since March 4, 1933. But behind that voluminous account of our salvation lies another vital chapter in American history.

This book surveys major developments touching American economics and politics between the summer of 1932 and the February-March paralysis of 1933. It is an attempt to weave into ordered chronology those controlling events at home and abroad which culminated, after four heartening months of solid world recovery, in a new American collapse.

It is the account of a Washington eye-witness, buttressed and illumed by the findings of a score or more of professional observers in the watchtowers of journalism, business, and finance. Under all lie the official documents now available from several governmental agencies.

Had the economic spiral of deflation and World War liquidation swept unchecked from the financial collapse in Central Europe, in the spring of 1931, to complete international prostration in the early months of 1933, the whole picture would have been subject to interpretation in its own terms. But the 1933 banking suspension in the United States was purely a national phenomenon. It was not a segment of the world charts. Our downward plunge through January-March was distinctly against the long-term economic indices in every other considerable country. Somewhere, somehow, a chain of events purely local to the United States pulled us out of the tide of world recovery and swept us into new shoals of panic and disaster. Were these destructive forces chiefly political, economic, financial, or only psychological? Does the period offer guidance for the future?

The banking crisis was, of course, a many-sided monster. Even today, it presents to every vantage point, a new face of horror. Our vantage point in January, February, and March, 1933, was the White House.

Through the telephones of the White House press room flowed news of every major development in the crisis. Cabinet officers, Under-Secretaries, Federal Reserve officials, and bankers from every section of the country were in and out of the Executive Offices from morning until midnight; Congressional leaders of every political and economic stripe figured in the many proposals put forward during February in Washington's heroic effort to avert disaster. The daily press conferences of the President or the Secretary of the Treasury, buttressed as they often were by interviews with Senators, Representatives, and members of the Federal Reserve Board as they passed, afforded the White House news corps an impressive hour-to-hour account of the national conflagration as it spread.

Since March, 1933, a considerable volume of documentary material and personal narrative has illumed many murky corners of the scene. President Roosevelt has treated various phases of the pre-inaugural developments in two books; in *The Challenge to Liberty*, former President Hoover illuminates several pivotal episodes; from Mr. Ernest K. Lindley's *The Roosevelt Revolution* we have an abridged account of several decisive events in New York, Albany, Hyde Park, Warm Springs, and aboard the *Nourmahal*. From official sources Mr. Mark Sullivan has published the story of the European gold crisis of 1931, particularly as it involved American policy and action, and as it unleashed violent new pressures upon American banking. More recently, Mr. Irwin H. Hoover's memoirs have provided an intimate account of the pre-inaugural meetings between President Hoover and President-elect Roosevelt, and Mr. Theodore G. Joslin has flashed upon the screen of history a series of vivid moments at President Hoover's desk. Finally, Mr. Herbert Hoover has published his private correspondence with the President-elect.

Books by Mr. James P. Warburg and Mr. Frank A. Vanderlip,

and magazine articles by Mr. Bernard Baruch and General Hugh S. Johnson, also have lighted some cloudy spots in the chronology of February, 1933, particularly with reference to the projected policies of the then incoming Administration.

Equally important as original source material are the records of the Senate Banking and Currency Committee's inquiry into the Detroit suspension; the record of the Michigan investigation of the same episode; the official publications of the Federal Reserve Board relating to the national suspension and resumption, particularly the annual reports for 1932 and 1933. Also, there have been published two illuminating reports of the Economic Policy Committee of the American Bankers' Association, one on the functioning of the Federal Reserve system during the panic, the other on *Banking After the Crisis*. Additional material of genuine historical significance since has been made available in the monthly and annual reports of the Reconstruction Finance Corporation, and in the proceedings of the American Bankers' Association.

All this voluminous material, which is catalogued in the bibliography (page 121) has been surveyed by the author, patterned here in the light of personal notes and diary entries preserved from the White House and Treasury conferences of January, February, and March, 1933.

Many gaps in the story since have been spanned by personal exchanges with principals—government officials, bankers, Senators, and Members of the House of Representatives—who participated in the daily White House conferences during the crisis, but none of these individuals, of course, shares in any degree the author's responsibility for conclusions drawn from the material at hand.

In the text, secondary names are presented only as they appear in official documents now available in the public record.

Throughout his months of study, and in the preparation of the manuscript, the author has sought only to present in calm and orderly perspective a series of momentous events which, because of their very sweep and intensity, thus far have remained wholly without historical pattern.

L. S.

*Chevy Chase, Md.*
*September, 1936.*

# CONTENTS

# CHAPTER I

## THE BREATH OF RECOVERY

REPUTABLE economic opinion appears to have crystallized upon the conviction that England's abandonment of gold, in September, 1931, signalized the beginning of the most violent phase of the secondary post-war depression. That blow shook the international financial structure to its very foundations, for the fall of the pound—a presumably impregnable standard of value and exchange in every market place of the world—was more than a terrific economic shock to commercial and investment confidence. It was a blow which shook the *spirit* of the world. "As safe as the Bank of England" long had been a by-word of security in times of stress. If this security could tumble, then, indeed, every other value must be tested anew. Only herculean measures enabled America to escape collapse in the international gold panic which followed.

The accelerated downward spiral of world economy from September, 1931, until the late spring of 1932 is ample evidence of the severity of this final testing of values. But for the United States the period was particularly distressing. Our spiritual and psychological exhaustion after two years of ever-expanding depression long since had become the central factor in commercial and speculative forecasts the world around. With the fall of the pound, our close financial and commercial ties with Great Britain focused upon us the central beam of the world's darkest doubts and misgivings. Everywhere men asked, "Will America topple too?"

In two successive sweeps of international panic, extending over eight months, this country gave up $1,200,000,000 in gold—more than one-fourth of her holdings—and saw her metallic reserves fall to the lowest point in ten years. Simultaneously, domestic hoarding of currency expanded our monetary circulation by a little more than $1,000,000,000. Every dollar of this hoarded money was backed by the statutory 40 per cent gold reserve. The resultant strain of these two mutually aggravating forces upon the American banking structure was such that, for a time in February, 1932, the combined reserves of all Federal Reserve member banks were

1

within $50,000,000 of the minimum permitted by law.[1] No other single fact, I believe, presents so vividly the gravity of the world situation at the trough of the depression.

The following paragraph from the *Annual Report* of the Federal Reserve Board for 1932 (published May 4, 1933) epitomizes the crisis which confronted the United States a year before the banking suspension:

On February 24, 1932, the Federal Reserve Banks had $1,392,000,000 of excess reserves, but as they did not have a sufficient amount of eligible paper available as collateral, $930,000,000 of these excess reserves in the form of gold had to be pledged as collateral against Federal Reserve notes, in addition to $46,000,000 required for the redemption fund, with the consequence that the gold not needed for these purposes amounted to $416,000,000.

But as a charge against this $416,000,000 there was an item of approximately $800,000,000 in foreign balances accumulated in the United States. Of these balances the same report of the Federal Reserve Board said:

The situation was further complicated by the fact that, notwithstanding the large withdrawals of foreign funds which had occurred in the autumn of 1931, foreign central banks still had a large volume of short term balances in this country, which were subject to withdrawal on demand, and which there was reason to believe would be withdrawn in large part in the course of a few months.

Not only were foreign balances withdrawn in this period of siege, but millions of dollars in foreign investments also were converted into American gold balances; and for a time these additional accumulations were being shipped as fast as ocean bottoms became available. Besides testing America's gold position, the tremendous liquidation of foreign security accounts on our great exchanges helped beat prices down to panic levels. The resultant impairment of domestic investment portfolios threatened the solvency of every bank, insurance company and fiduciary agency in the land. Here, indeed, America stood on the brink of default—and had she toppled at this point the financial machinery of the entire world would have fallen in utter paralysis.

Into this perilous situation President Hoover threw the Glass-Steagall Act of February 27, 1932. It authorized the substitution

---

[1] Federal Reserve Board, Annual Report 1932.

of government bonds for commercial paper under the Federal Reserve circulation, and thus released some $700,000,000 in reserve gold as a bulwark against the panic demand from abroad. In the sixty-day period May 5 to July 6, 1932, government securities used as collateral under this act reached a peak of $682,000,000.[2]

In thus appraising the work of this emergency legislation, it may be observed parenthetically that the Glass-Steagall authority, formally recommended by the President on December 6, 1931— after having been outlined in detail to the banking committee leaders of the House and Senate early in October—was not enacted into law until February 27, 1932. Senator Carter Glass, of Virginia, without whose support and approval no banking legislation could be passed in the Seventy-second Congress, did not abandon his opposition to the Glass-Steagall bill until he had been convinced, at a five-hour White House "breakfast conference" late in February, that without the measure America, too, soon would be compelled to default on gold demands.

Against such legislative obstruction President Hoover, of course, was virtually powerless, for any public appeal based upon an official presentation of the American position at the moment could have had no other effect than to precipitate at once the world calamity all were striving to avert. By its very nature it had to be a fight behind the scenes.

But with the passage of the Glass-Steagall Act every demand from abroad was met. Gradually the international gold run subsided. The heavy foreign withdrawals ended in July, 1932, and in August the return movement began. Twice during this period of recurrent international panic, however—first in October, 1931, and again in May-June, 1932—the world saw gold movements on a scale previously unknown in history.

Meanwhile, the American financial structure had been bolstered by the operations of the National Credit Corporation and the Reconstruction Finance Corporation. The Credit Corporation, hastily organized at a White House conference in October, 1931, saved hundreds of scattered banking situations during the last quarter of that year and the first days of 1932. Its capital of $500,-000,000 had been subscribed by the principal banks of the country,

---

[2] Federal Reserve Board, Annual Report, 1932.

with a firm agreement between the financial community and President Hoover, from the October conferences in Washington, that if further credits proved necessary strong measures for governmental action would be submitted to the Congress in December.

Pursuant to this agreement the Reconstruction Finance Corporation was recommended in the President's message to Congress on December 6, 1931. The bill was enacted in the last weeks of January, 1932. Beginning operations on February 2, the R.F.C. made loans of $1,400,000,000 through June. Together, these three measures—the National Credit Corporation, the Glass-Steagall Act, and the R.F.C.—maintained American solvency in the face of the most terrific international gold run in history. Unquestionably, this defense of the dollar stands as the most gigantic piece of economic statesmanship ever accomplished under the forms of representative government.

During March and April, 1932, when this battle was at its height, two smashing episodes in the world news sent sharp currents of unanticipated shock through the American financial system. The first was the suicide, in Paris, of Ivar Kreuger, which exposed an undreamed web of fantastic speculative pyramiding in international finance. The second was the collapse of the Insull utility empire in the Middle West. By wiping out tens of thousands of small investors in America, and by further assaulting public confidence in banks and investment, these two financial crashes carried the country once more to the very brink of a general money panic. The R.F.C. caught the bobble. Yet the fact remains that these added strains came at a moment when those directing the battle in Washington believed that every weapon and every resource of American economy already had been thrown into the lists.

Moreover, at about this point a third distressing aggravation of our domestic situation developed in Congress. As banking pressures became acute from time to time, a considerable group of influential Democratic leaders in the House of Representatives gave public support to the inevitable clamor for monetary inflation. A fiat-money bill, carrying the volatile soldiers' bonus for political propulsion, was passed in the House and sent to the Senate. New demands for prodigious boot-strap spending by the Federal Government were pressed in both House and Senate. Simultaneously, unblushing partisan obstruction in both Houses made legislative mincemeat of President Hoover's program for a balanced budget.[a]

Under these political excitements the pressure of hoarding, domestic gold withdrawals, and frightened liquidation of bond and stock assets swept onward through May and June, 1932. When, early in June, President Hoover appeared unexpectedly before the Senate, to urge immediate action on the long-delayed tax bill, foreign gold withdrawals again were approaching $100,-000,000 a *week!* Although this fact was not stated in the President's special message, there were, in his urgent pleas against continued political obstruction, unmistakable hints of an extremely grave condition. The billion-dollar tax bill of 1932 was passed by the Senate next day.

With the defeat of all threatening inflationary legislation in June and the adjournment of Congress at mid-July—which coincided with the complete restoration of foreign confidence in the American gold position—the breath of recovery began to be felt over the land.

## TABLE I

*Net Change in American Gold*

| | |
|---|---:|
| September, 1931 | + $20,561,000 |
| October | − 337,685,000 |
| November | + 89,436,000 |
| December | + 56,858,000 |
| January, 1932 | − 72,950,000 |
| February | − 90,567,000 |
| March | − 24,671,000 |
| April | − 30,239,000 |
| May | − 195,514,000 |
| June | − 206,047,000 |
| July | − 3,437,000 |
| August | + 6,103,000 |
| September | + 27,898,000 |
| October | + 20,613,000 |
| November | + 21,740,000 |
| December | + 100,859,000 |

+ indicates net imports.
− indicates net exports.

---

[a] The legislative history of the 1931 budget program is sketched in Chapter V.

The tabulation of net gold movements to and from the United States, (Table I), compiled from weekly reports of the Federal Reserve Board, presents vividly the complete cycle of the unprecedented international panic here so successfully weathered.

As the tide of acute panic subsided in June-July, 1932—and this coincided, as it happened, with the Republican and Democratic national conventions at Chicago—the business curves turned upward in every major industrial country in the world. Chart I graphically illustrates this sharp turning of the world tide from depression to recovery.

Observe that the upturn which began at about the middle of 1932 held firmly in England, France, Germany, Italy, Belgium, and Japan through the first quarter of 1933. But in the United States this upward surge was done to death, and March, 1933, found us below the world trough of July, 1932.

The specific acts of political sabotage in and out of Congress which contributed to this isolated reversal of the recovery tide in the United States will be examined in detail in succeeding chapters. But first let us examine hastily the general nature and specific details of our domestic recovery during the summer of 1932.

Confirming the world graph plotted in Chart I by Mr. Leonard P. Ayres of the Cleveland Trust Company, is an equally significant study from the League of Nations' *World Economic Survey, 1932-33,* representing world prices and raw material stocks.

Showing a steadily increasing accumulation of raw materials until the summer of 1932, Chart II clearly marks the basic economic improvement which then took hold. At this juncture world stocks began to diminish—evidence of fundamental economic adjustment—and the consolidated long-sweep curve of world prices turned upward for the first time in three and one-half years.

Throughout the United States this turn was reflected in every field of our economic life. In the stock market, the barometer of national psychology as well as of economic values, the Standard Statistics index of 351 industrial stocks swept from a low of 34 in early July to a high of 56 in September (in relatives of the 1926 base of 100). On the New York Stock Exchange, leading industrial issues doubled in price, while rail shares nearly trebled. The

## CHART I

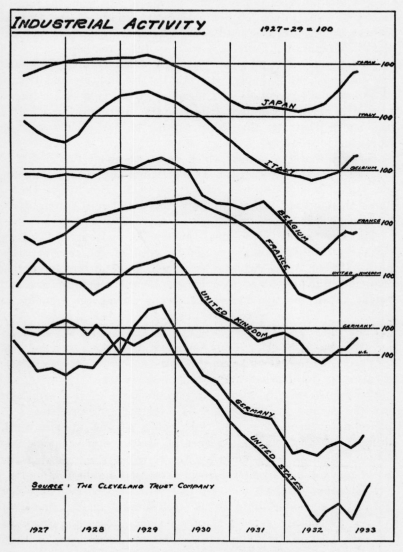

At about June, 1932, the composite industrial index turned upward strongly in every major country of the world. Only the United States lost this recovery of the last half of the year.

CHART II

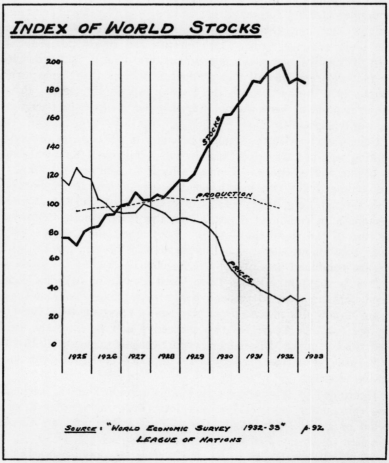

*Combined world stocks of raw materials began to decline at mid-year 1932.*

Standard Bond Index bounded up from 72.2 for June to 85.8 for September. The weighted average of seventeen New York bank stocks advanced from a depression low of $31.34 per share on May 31 to $70.76 on September 7, the 1932 high. The close December 31 was $58.95.[4]

---

[4] Hoit, Rose & Troster report, January, 1933.

In the sharp reversal of market sentiment which followed the September election forecast from Maine, and continued generally through February, 1933, stocks on the big board lost more than half their summer gains. But neither the industrial nor rail averages again touched the depression lows of July, 1932, despite the fact that commercial and production indices in February and March, 1933, broke through the lows of April-July, 1932. From whatever point of view, July, 1932, recorded the extreme trough of the world depression.

Concurrently with the summer recovery in the security markets, banking regained its equilibrium in every important financial center of the United States. Domestic bank suspensions (all banks) had averaged 209 per month for the eleven months September, 1931, through July, 1932, with an average freezing of $144,378,000 per month in combined deposits. In the three months following the turn of the world tide—August, September, and October, 1932 —our total bank suspensions averaged only 85 per month, with average combined deposits of $21,038,000.

Nor is that all. During these three months of recovery combined deposits released through bank resumptions *exceeded* those frozen in new suspensions by an average of approximately $8,000,-000 per month. Never for two successive months since the 1929 crash had resumed deposits exceeded deposits suspended. In the 1932 turn the excess of deposit resumptions ruled for four successive months.

Heartened by this nation-wide stabilization in finance, the business community began to venture forth once more, after a long period of credit siege, hand-to-mouth operations, and an almost complete suspensions of capital investment.

Wholesale commodity prices and farm prices advanced steadily through July and August, and held the gains through September.

The Federal Reserve Board's index of industrial production swept upward from 56 in July to 68 for both September and October.

United States cotton manufacturing leaped from 51.5 percent of mill capacity in July to 97 percent in October. Domestic wool consumption advanced from 16,500,000 pounds in May to 46,100,-000 pounds in September.

The American Federation of Labor reported 12,300,000 unemployed on July 1, and 11,586,000 on October 1. The August,
1932 review of the Department of Labor showed the first upturn
in seasonally adjusted indices of factory employment and payrolls
since the spring of 1931. The August industrial review of *The
Annalist* reported "the first advance of any magnitude since April,
1931."

The construction industries, as reflected in the Federal Reserve
Board's index of contracts awarded, improved fractionally from
approximately 25 percent to 33 percent of the 1923-25 normal.
Adjusted for seasonal variations, *The Annalist* index of residential
construction for September showed "the first upturn of even such
small proportions since January, 1931."

Tracing the same movement in retail trade, the Federal Reserve Board's seasonally adjusted index of department store sales
moved upward from 67 in July to 71 in October, a level not
recorded again until August, 1933.

Electric power production hit the 1932 low in July, at 6,112,-
000,000 kilowatt hours, and then registered consistent monthly advances through October. But the October figure of 6,633,000,000
kilowatt hours was not matched again until June, 1933.

Freight car loadings advanced from an average of 80,000 cars
daily early in July, 1932, to 96,000 cars daily during the first two
weeks of October.

The September backlog of the United States Steel Corporation
was the first in sixteen months to show an increase over the previous month.

Moody reported net earnings of 63 principal railroads in the
third quarters of 1932 as 95 percent above the second quarter.

Sixteen dominant petroleum companies showed net earnings of
$18,652,000 for the first nine months of 1932, against a combined
deficit of $41,848,000 in the corresponding months of 1931.

Dun and Bradstreet's index of business failures fell off precipi-
tately through August and September.

Noting better production schedules in textiles, shoes, clothing,
coal, steel, increased car loadings, and firmly rising wholesale
prices, the September employment survey of the American Fed-

CHART III

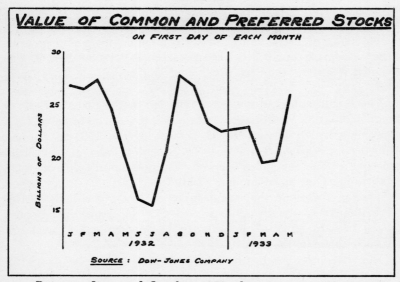

VALUE OF COMMON AND PREFERRED STOCKS

ON FIRST DAY OF EACH MONTH

SOURCE : DOW-JONES COMPANY

*Between June and October 1932, the aggregate value of all
stocks listed on the New York Stock Exchange nearly doubled.
After the election, half of these gains were lost in fears of gold
abandonment, dollar devaluation, and inflation.*

eration of Labor dwelt at some length upon "signs of real business improvement."

After a struggle which had left ugly wounds and scars on all,
we were actually coming over the hill. The warm breath of recovery stirred again in the land of the locust.

Reviewing other voluminous recovery data of 1932, Mr. Walter
Lippmann, in November, 1933, presented the conclusion—

There is very good statistical evidence which goes to prove that as a
purely economic phenomenon the world depression reached its low point
in the mid-summer of 1932, and that in all the leading countries a very
slow but nevertheless real recovery began.[5]

Similarly, Mr. Leonard P. Ayres, in surveying this four-month
period of world restoration in 1932, summarized American developments thus:

[5] New York Herald-Tribune, November 14, 1933.

This country is now [June 1933] participating in a general recovery of industrial activity that was initiated abroad. Our industries joined in the upturn last summer, and carried the gains forward to the close of the year [1932]. Then political dissensions and banking troubles combined to cause a new decline.

The records of other nations suggest that an adequate remedy might have been found if the prompt and vigorous actions taken had been directed to restoring full confidence in our banking system. In that event our present business upturn and speculation would probably have been less violent, but possibly our general recovery more durable.

CHART IV

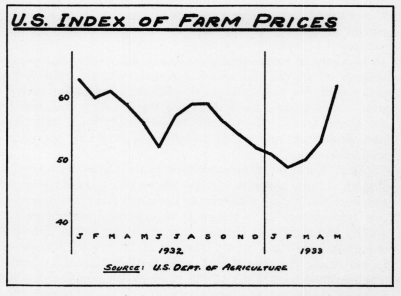

*The composite index of United States farm prices advanced notably in the summer of 1932, strongly against the normal seasonal trend. All these gains were lost, however, following the election, and the level of September, 1932, was not attained again until April, 1933.*

# Chapter II

# POLITICAL INTERLUDE

**E**VEN in periods of relative stability our presidential campaign
sometimes becomes a controlling factor in national business
sentiment during the summer and fall of election year. The national estimate of the convention nominees, the appraisal of prospective policies, and the hazards of a post-election interregnum of
uncertainty—all these considerations may tend to restrain expansion and postpone great plans and projects.[1]

At the same time, the political lightning and campaign thunder
almost inevitably project successive ripples of public excitement
or alarm; and there is always the danger, even if often remote,
that one of these spasms of enthusiasm or indignation may get out
of control and send large segments of the population off in wild
pursuit of lo here! and lo there! or into some blind hysteria of
conduct.

In years of extraordinary economic dislocation this cautious
attitude of the political sounding period quite naturally is more
pronounced; for in such times the dangers of ravishing sweeps of
irrational mob psychosis usually are aggravated by inflammatory
demagogic appeal. To the professional politician of the opposition, defamation and public incitement always offer the path of
least resistance.

Thus, it was the unfortunate fate of the United States in 1932
that all of these abnormal stresses and strains of presidential politics were set in play precisely at the turn of the world economic
tide from depression to recovery, at a moment when civil tranquillity and individual freedom from fears and alarms offered the
one great hope for a steady advance of the recovery movement.
In one sense, presidential campaigns may be likened to football.
The smashing hurly-burly of the skirmish is stimulating to beefy
linesmen in the pink of physical condition. But it does not follow
that football is a wholesome recovery regime for the feebly convalescent typhoid patient.

When the party conventions presented their national tickets

---

[1] Chart movements in 1924 provide a particularly clear and striking example
of this phenomenon.

13

in June and July, 1932, the United States was a figurative convalescent—just beginning to hobble about again after a three-years siege of fallen everything.

And at this point, destiny touched the patient on the shoulder and told him to take his place in the center of the line!

In view of the economic situation which prevailed at the beginning of the campaign, every event or action which distracted or restrained the feebly stirring recuperative energies of the nation came as a direct thrust at the public welfare. Insofar as such distractions flowed from premeditated assaults upon reviving public confidence demagogic political stratagems became, in the historical view, starkly treasonable.

President Hoover's policies, as proclaimed in two and a half years of unremitting battle against world forces of economic disintegration, were well known to the country. They pivoted upon the defense of constitutional processes, maintenance of sound money, efficiently administered relief of human distress, an unceasing fight for an honestly balanced budget, protection of the national financial structure against panic and hysteria, and a program of sincere international collaboration for the effective organization of recovery and the peace of the world. He had pressed for the development of agencies for the prevention of bankruptcy and foreclosure upon homes and farms, and had urged needed reforms in banking, finance, and business methods.

Despite an antagonistic Congress, he had built up public works, and spread work; organized the country against distress as a local responsibility supplemented with Federal support; strengthened the Farm Loan System; created the Agricultural Credit Banks, the Home Loan Banking system, the Reconstruction Finance Corporation; encouraged a large movement of sound credit expansion through the Reserve system; held the gold standard impregnable from foreign attack; lessened the strain on the world by the moratorium on intergovernmental debts, which led to the Lausanne Conference; had taken a large part in the initiation of a world conference on stabilization of currencies and the reduction of trade barriers; had increased taxes, and but for increasing relief expenditure, had reduced expenses until a balanced budget actually was in sight with moderate recovery.[2]

---

[2] For details of Mr. Hoover's 1933-34 budget, see Chapter V.

Under all these policies lay the foundation stone of firm adherence to the deep traditions of American life—to the fundamental concepts of individual liberty and ordered freedom under law.

"Through it all," President Hoover said in his acceptance address in Washington on August 11, 1932, "our first duty is to preserve unfettered that dominant American spirit which has produced our enterprise and individual character. That is the bed rock of the past, and that is the guaranty of the future. Not regimented mechanisms but free men is our goal. Herein is the fundamental issue: a representative Democracy, progressive and unafraid to meet its problems, but meeting them upon the foundations of experience and not upon the wave of emotion, or the insensate demands of a radicalism which grasps at every opportunity to exploit the sufferings of a people."

Thrice recalling the historic tendency of democracies in the presence of national dangers "to strike blindly, to listen to demagogues and slogans," President Hoover concluded his acceptance address on the earnest note: "I shall seek to maintain untarnished and unweakened those fundamental traditions and principles upon which our nation was founded and upon which it has grown."

On the other side of the political arena, the nomination of Franklin D. Roosevelt and John N. Garner in the Democratic National Convention, early in July, had served notice on all men of national perception that the opposition campaign probably would be pitched to a rousing appeal in behalf of "the Forgotten Man." Nevertheless, the overwhelming acclaim which greeted President Hoover's acceptance address in August offered momentary assurance that the national morale yet would withstand the anticipated three months' appeal of ambitious opportunism.

Presumably the positive economic policies of the Democratic nominees would be stated in the campaign; but meanwhile the nation could anticipate that party's program only in the light of the public records of the nominees.

Because of his conduct in the first session of the Seventy-second Congress, then drawing to a close, Speaker Garner was the principal concern of all those who clocked the pulse of recovery.

As Speaker of the House of Representatives since December, 1931, Mr. Garner had covertly obstructed the Hoover economic program by every means at the command of that high parliamentary office. And yet, by repeated public professions of sincere non-partisan co-operation he had successfully concealed his sabotage from the public view. For this reason the profound political significance of his nomination at Chicago was lost to the public at large. Few people outside of Washington grasp the complexities of parliamentary law or the subtleties of party control in Congress. Not one person in a hundred throughout the country, therefore, realized as he read of Mr. Garner's nomination at Chicago that the Speaker, while professedly supporting every measure of economic defense presented in Congress during a period of supreme national trial, actually had resisted many of them. Secret obstruction, parliamentary sniping and demagogic distortion of policies and purposes had been his weapons. Using them expertly he had played them with devastating effect upon virtually every measure of reconstruction to the very closing days of the session, at mid-July—two weeks after his nomination as vice-president. The clause requiring publication of all R.F.C. loans, Mr. Garner's great triumph of the session, was written into an emergency relief bill on July 16, 1932.

Although President Hoover and every agency of government charged with financial administration warned of the dangers of this publicity policy, Mr. Garner regarded it as a signal personal achievement. En route to his Texas home after the adjournment, he stopped briefly at Dallas to greet a station audience.

"I hold the most powerful position in the government excepting that of President of the United States," he said on that occasion. "I accepted the proposed vice-presidential nomination with much hesitancy, for already we had whipped Hoover three times in Congress."

Reviewing the celebrated "pork-barrel" fight over the 1932 federal relief bill, Mr. Garner continued:

I trusted the President enough to be willing to leave the distribution of that money to his judgment, but he called it a pork-barrel measure. Then, because I demanded that the R.F.C. make public its use of $2,000,-000,000 of the people's property, he said, in effect, "No, that is for the benefit of my select clientele, and the people must not know what is done with it." Well, we passed that measure anyway!

I notice by the morning papers that he says he will study it a few days and probably will sign it. He means he wants to have a few days in which to find out what Wall Street and J. P. Morgan think he should do about it.

This heady blast of precinct chatter from a vice-presidential nominee, and directed to the person of the President of the United States, shocked the nation. It was greeted by an instant roar of editorial condemnation from both the Democratic and Republican press. The Speaker did not speak again until late September.

The next occasion for a public utterance from him was in connection with Mr. Roosevelt's address of September 29, at Sioux City, Iowa, which demanded a sharp reduction in the number of bureaus and commissions in Washington, and drastic curtailment of the national tax burden. Interviewed at Washington next day, Speaker Garner said in part:

> Governor Roosevelt's Sioux City speech struck direct to the roots of the evils responsible for existing economic conditions and cannot fail to impress all those whose minds are open to sound logic. His statements in reference to economy in governmental expenditures will be of special interest to the over-burdened taxpayer, and his assertion that the President has the right, and even the duty, of taking moral leadership in bringing about a reduction of state and local taxes as well as those of the federal government, will strike a responsive chord throughout the country.

These two utterances and one brief radio address constituted Mr. Garner's major public effort in the 1932 campaign. They are interesting historically only for the light they throw on the violent personal impulses to public excitement which motivated the Democratic vice-presidential nominee, both in his capacity as a candidate and as Speaker of the House of Representatives.

Although Mr. Roosevelt had been a national figure in his party since his nomination for the vice-presidency in 1920, his views on the great issues confronting the nation in 1932 were unknown. Some trained political observers had been given concern by his somewhat vacuous pre-convention appeal in behalf of "the Forgotten Man."

One warning of this had come from Alfred E. Smith at the Jefferson Day dinner in Washington, on April 14, 1932.

"This is no time for demagogues," Mr. Smith shouted vehemently before the boisterous acclaim of his partisan audience.

> At a time like this, when millions of men and women and children are starving throughout the land, there is always the temptation to some men to stir up class prejudice, to stir up the bitterness of the rich against the poor and the poor against the rich.

Against that effort I set myself uncompromisingly. I protest against the endeavor to delude the poor people of this country to their ruin by trying to make them believe that they can get employment before the people who would ordinarily employ them are also again restored to conditions of normal prosperity.

A factory worker cannot get his job back until business conditions enable the factory owner to open up again; and to promise the great masses of the working people that they can secure renewed employment by class legislation is treachery to those working people, to the principles of the Democratic Party, and to this United States itself.

I have recently stated that while I would accept the nomination for the Presidency if it were tendered me by the convention, that until the convention assembled I would not be for or against any candidate. I announce tonight an exception to that statement. I will take off my coat and fight to the end against any candidate who persists in any demagogic appeal to the masses of the working people of this country to destroy themselves by setting class against class and rich against poor.

Equally pointed on this score was a letter from Mr. Thomas L. Chadbourne, long an influential figure in the national councils of the Democratic Party, to Homer S. Cummings, the Connecticut manager of the Roosevelt pre-convention campaign. Early in March Mr. Cummings had solicited support for the Roosevelt boom. Mr. Chadbourne's reply was quoted at length in the *New York Times* for April 25, 1932, as follows:

Since your letter of March 2, asking as to my feelings about the movement to nominate Governor Roosevelt, and my answer to you of March 30 (delayed on account of my absence in Cuba) stating that while I "always liked Frank" I was not in a position to study the nomination situation on account of illness, the Governor has made two speeches.

The first (of April 7) shocked me unspeakably. It convicted him of a cheap opportunism bordering on downright demagogy. In that speech he betrayed a willingness to play upon the irritations, suspicions, and bitterness of these troubled and unhappy times. Such an unconstructive attack as he there indulged in can have no possible object except political advantage, and at the present moment, when cooperative effort is the command of patriotism, such attacks are terribly hurtful, adding to confusion and futility.

As one who has remained a Democrat against the continuous pressure of a hostile environment, and as a devoted follower of Woodrow Wilson and an unswerving supporter of all his reforms that struck at special privilege and made for equal justice, and as one who has devoted much of his time and income for years, as President of the American Association for Labor Legislation, to efforts to ameliorate the conditions of labor, I make bold to call myself a progressive Democrat. What I deeply resent, however, is the fake progressivism that has its base in the incitement of mob anger and the capitalization of mass unhappiness and crowd despairs.

Many and fundamental changes will have to be made in the established order of things. A first task, however, is to meet present emergencies. When a dike breaks, intelligent men concentrate upon repairing the break, waiting until ,a later and safer time to discuss plans for changing and strengthening the system as a whole. Either Frank Roosevelt is without enough common sense to grasp these simplicities, or else he chooses deliberately to disregard them, putting his own ambition above the common good.

In the past twenty years you and I have fought shoulder to shoulder and have pretty much always seen four-square politically. I am sorry it cannot be so this time. . . .

But far overshadowing such intimate appraisals of the candidates was the larger, and controlling, public impression created by the unequivocal sound-money plank and the firm promise of a balanced budget in the Democratic national platform.

That platform, it will be recalled by some, did not offer a revolution *per se*. Nor did it give any hint that constitutional processes might be abandoned in both legislation and administration. Granted, then, the perfectly natural assumption that in the long view the fundamental concepts of American life were to guide both parties, the immediate recovery concerns of the country at the outset of the campaign were only two; first, sound money, and second, a balanced federal budget.

True, there were in the business and financial community, despite the platform, widespread misgivings concerning Democratic intentions on these two points. Under Mr. Garner's leadership the House of Representatives, in the Spring of 1932, had passed the Patman fiat-money bonus bill, the Goldsborough commodity-dollar bill, and the billion-dollar Wagner-Garner loan and construction bill.[3] Between April and mid-July, 1932, these and other easy-money measures in the House had inspired throughout the country genuine alarms of inflation. But with sound money and governmental economy now firmly imbedded in the Democratic platform, and with that platform accepted "100 per cent" by Mr. Roosevelt, such fears were vastly diminished. By and large, the choice of the electorate as between the two parties was reasonably presumed by all, at this point, to lie in the field of personal approach and administrative details. It was on this basis that the historic campaign began.

Nor were the solemn party pledges on sound money and a bal-

---

[3] Only the latter measure passed the Senate, and it was drastically modified after President Hoover's veto.

anced budget forgotten during the campaign. Senator Carter
Glass of Virginia, a former Secretary of the Treasury, and recognized nationally as an uncompromising foe of currency manipulation, nailed both pledges to the mast in a nation-wide radio
broadcast late in October. And at Brooklyn, on November 4, Mr.
Roosevelt himself further bolstered the money plank with this
unequivocal language:

The business men of the country, battling hard to maintain their
financial solvency and integrity, were told in blunt language in Des Moines,
Iowa, how close an escape the country had some months ago from going
off the gold standard. This, as has been fairly shown since, was a libel on
the credit of the United States.

No adequate answer has been made to that magnificent philippic of
Senator Glass the other night, in which he showed how unsound was this
assertion. And I might add, Senator Glass made a devastating challenge
that no responsible government would have sold to the country securities
payable in gold if it knew that the promise, yes, the covenant, embodied
in these securities was as dubious as the President of the United States
claims it was. Of course, the assertion was unsound.

From this specious pledge to preserve the gold standard, Mr.
Roosevelt turned directly to currency, continuing:

One of the most commonly repeated misrepresentations by Republican
speakers, including the President, has been the claim that the Democratic
position with regard to money has not been made sufficiently clear. The
President is seeing visions of rubber dollars. This is only a part of his
campaign of fear. I am not going to characterize these statements. I
merely present the facts.

The Democratic platform specifically declares, "We advocate a sound
currency to be preserved at all hazards." That is plain English.

In discussing this platform on July 30, I said, "Sound money is an
international necessity, not a domestic consideration for one nation alone."

Far up in the Northwest, at Butte, I repeated the pledge of the platform, saying, "Sound currency must be maintained at all regards."

In Seattle I reaffirmed my attitude on this question. The thing has
been said, therefore, in plain English three times in my speeches. It is
stated without qualification in the platform, and I have announced my
unqualified acceptance of that platform.

So much for that misrepresentation.

If, three days before election, anyone still harbored doubts as to
Mr. Roosevelt's determination to avoid the dangers of currency
management, he might have turned again to the Democratic
national platform and read:

We believe that a party platform is a covenant with the people to be
faithfully kept by the party when entrusted with power, and that the
people are entitled to know in plain words the terms of the contract to
which they are asked to subscribe.

And for details of this covenant the citizen might also have read:

> We advocate an immediate and drastic reduction of governmental expenditures by abolishing useless commissions and offices, consolidating departments and bureaus, and eliminating extravagance to accomplish a saving of not less than 25 per cent in the cost of Federal Government. . . . We favor maintenance of the national credit by a federal budget annually balanced on the basis of accurate executive estimates within revenues. . . . We advocate a sound currency to be maintained at all hazards. . . . We advocate unemployment and old-age insurance under state laws. . . . We advocate strengthening and impartial enforcement of the anti-trust laws, to prevent monopoly and unfair trade practices, and the revision thereof for the better protection of labor and the small producer and distributor . . . the removal of government from all fields of private enterprise except where necessary to develop public works and natural resources in the common interest. . . . We advocate quicker methods of realizing on assets for relief of depositors of suspended banks. . . . We oppose cancellation of debts owing to the United States by foreign nations. . . . We condemn . . . the unsound policy of restricting agricultural products to the demands of domestic markets.

In the face of these strong pledges in defense of the American political system, who could share Republican alarms over the promise of the New Deal? Here it was, black on white, sound, unequivocal, progressive, statesmanlike in brevity and clarity.

For a considerable section of national opinion, nevertheless, there persisted throughout the entire campaign grave doubts as to Mr. Roosevelt's real intentions regarding money. How well founded were these doubts was demonstrated a year later, when Mr. Ernest K. Lindley's *The Roosevelt Revolution* came from the presses with the whole story of Mr. Roosevelt's campaign strategy on the money issue. Said Mr. Lindley, at page 36:

> The points on which Mr. Roosevelt specifically strove to reassure the conservatives were the balancing of the budget by drastic governmental economies and the preservation of sound money. Yet, adhering to the pattern of the Democratic platform, Mr. Roosevelt at no time said that by sound money he meant the existing gold content of the dollar. He heartily lauded the scathing attack of Senator Glass on the Republican Administration . . . but he did not define sound money.
> The conservatives naturally assumed he meant a dollar of the existing gold content, and Mr. Roosevelt undoubtedly was glad to have them think so without completely quashing the hopes of the inflationists of various schools. In retrospect, the loopholes which Mr. Roosevelt left for himself in handling the money issue become significant. They indicate at least a mental reservation concerning the possibility or desirability of maintaining the existing gold standard.

Again touching this subject in another connection, Mr. Lindley explains on page 64 of the same work:

Mr. Roosevelt, as we have seen, had at least a mental reservation as to the possibility or desirability of maintaining the gold standard. But he could not admit it, or even hint at it, except in the most intimate circle of tight-lipped friends. Only a hint that he contemplated departure from the gold standard and he would have instantly caused the catastrophe that everyone wished to avoid.

Thus, it appears to be established that Mr. Roosevelt, himself, recognized from the very beginning that any announcement of his real intentions regarding gold and money involved some national risk, or, as Mr. Lindley interprets it, some risk of "the catastrophe that everyone wished to avoid."

Nor is this the only evidence that Mr. Roosevelt actually had begun to play with the idea of inflation long before he gave his strong campaign pledges to sound money. As early as mid-August, 1932, Mr. Henry A. Wallace, of Iowa, had visited Mr. Roosevelt at Albany. With the Democratic Presidential nominee was Professor Rexford Guy Tugwell, of Columbia University. Under date of August 29, Mr. Wallace wrote to Mr. George N. Peek: "Tugwell seems to have the inside track at the present time with Governor on economic matters. Tugwell is quite sold on the Domestic Allotment Plan, but he is against the honest dollar. Roosevelt is at heart, I believe, an inflationist, but I doubt if he says much about money affairs one way or another in this campaign."

It remains, therefore, a matter of profound historical significance that as of November 8, 1932, the nation at large, after a perfectly terrific campaign, had not the slightest intimation of the policies and programs actually in store at the hand of the victorious party.

Incredible as it may seem in retrospect, recovery advanced steadily from the conventions to the Maine elections in September. Here, the normal seasonal impulses came in to hold the gains—with many conflicting advances and recessions in various lines—until November. The "Brain Trust" had come into the political picture late in September, but even at election day nobody regarded it seriously as a prospective instrumentality of national administration.

It was the gradual revelation of the New Deal, in its own terms after the elections, which definitely reversed the tide of recovery and swept the nation into the dark chasm of the bank holiday.

CHAPTER III

THE NEW DEAL IN COMMAND

THE New Deal dominated the country, not from inauguration day on March 4, 1933, but from the day after election, or November 9, 1932. From that date the country awoke gradually to a wholly changed economic direction. Business hesitated for an appraisal of Mr. Roosevelt's prospective policies, for announcement of his Cabinet, for a clarification of his views on gold, money, international stabilization, war debts, and tariffs. Almost overnight, the strong forward surge of the recovery movement gave way to a new tempo of cautious sounding. No policy of the President-elect came into instant formal application, but the fact that his Party was in control of the House of Representatives made it highly improbable that any contrary policy might be enacted in the approaching short session of Congress. At best, therefore, a distressing period of uncertainty was in prospect, and at a moment when a robust national confidence was needed above all else to consolidate and sustain recovery.

Under this cloud of uncertainty, expansion orders were cancelled in many directions. New enterprises were held in abeyance. Manufacturers who feared a general reduction of tariffs began to run off accumulated stocks. Unemployment increased again in November and December.

Far overshadowing all these restraining impulses, however, was the great issue of money. Despite apparently sincere public assurances from Mr. Roosevelt on this score during the campaign, there were heard again immediately after the election repeated suggestions from the inflationists that the New Deal would bring some sort of new money. As these reports spread in the financial community, and were never stoutly denied by the President-elect, the primary symptoms of a distressing credit contraction began to appear. When there is doubt as the standard of the currency, no bank is sound. Gradually the symptoms of flight became apparent in the daily reports of the Comptroller of the Currency.

Precisely at this point the sudden emergence of the war debt problem forced the New Deal at once to the center of the world

23

CHART V

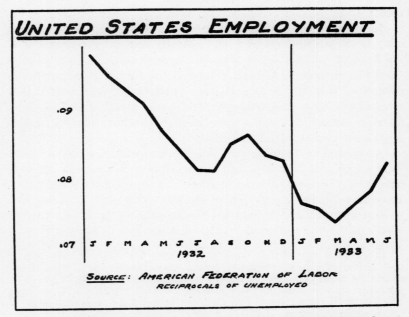

**UNITED STATES EMPLOYMENT**

.09

.08

.07    J F M A M J J A S O N D    J F M A M J J
                    *1932*                    *1933*

SOURCE: AMERICAN FEDERATION OF LABOR
RECIPROCALS OF UNEMPLOYED

*After three months of steady improvement against the normal seasonal trend, employment in the United States fell off in November 1932, to reach a new depression low during the banking holiday.*

stage—and in a way which served only to increase doubt concerning Mr. Roosevelt's philosophical attachment to the gold standard.

On November 10, 1932, two days after the election, the State Department was informed of a concerted movement by the principal European powers to seize upon the divided national leadership between election and inauguration as a promising opportunity to secure a reopening of the war debt agreements.

In July the Lausanne conference had practically wiped out the German reparations bill as embodied in the Young Agreements, but this had been done under a secret pact between our Allies providing that formal ratification of the cancellation should be contingent upon fully compensating adjustments of European debts to the United States. With the expiration of the Hoover moratorium of 1931, the next payments under the American debt agreements would be due December 15, 1932.

In these circumstances it was urgent that American policy at once be clearly defined and emphatically stated. An overwhelming flood of cancellation propaganda poured into the United States from the capitals of Europe. Some of the formal state communications of the debtor nations were published abroad before they reached our State Department. And a considerable section of influential American opinion gave itself enthusiastically to intensification of this cancellation drive.

A controlling factor in the American situation was the House rider which had been attached to the Hoover moratorium ratification in the Seventy-second Congress. This joint resolution, signed December 23, 1931, provided in the most emphatic language that no further executive concessions on the debt agreements would be sustained by the Congress. This language was unequivocal:

It is hereby expressly declared to be against the policy of the Congress that any of the indebtedness of foreign countries to the United States should be in any manner cancelled or reduced; and nothing in this joint resolution shall be construed as indicating a contrary policy or as implying that favorable consideration will be given at any time to a change in the policy hereby declared.

Inasmuch as this provision had been added to the ratification resolution under the personal leadership of Speaker Garner and Floor Leader Henry T. Rainey, and passed only with the votes of the Democratic majority in the House of Representatives, it was obvious that further debt negotiations by President Hoover alone in 1932 could accomplish nothing.

Moreover, with a change in government only four months ahead—and the prospect that any effective negotiations would extend far beyond that period—joint action between the outgoing and incoming administrations appeared inescapable. It appeared imperative that America should establish a continuing policy to bridge the inauguration, and that the new policy should be stated jointly by President Hoover and President-elect Roosevelt before December 15. Otherwise, the situation most certainly would drift into a general default on the December 15 payments, and this would mean the practical end of $11,000,000,000 of war debt obligations to the United States. Once a government has defaulted, no political party, nor any Cabinet leader, can survive the popular pressures against resumption. The *fait accompli* of default at once destroys all arguments for resumption. Here, then, was a problem of gigantic proportions to be acted upon decisively within thirty-five days.

But the debt issue did not stand alone in the critical posture of world affairs at November, 1932. The imperative cry for the stabilization of currencies and the removal of the choking artificial trade barriers which flowed directly from ever-increasing exchange difficulties, had been heard for many months.

Through a series of private conversations and diplomatic exchanges, President Hoover had arranged with Premier MacDonald that England should take the lead in calling a world economic conference. Plans had been made for the assembly of this conference in January, 1933, and President Hoover already had selected several members of the American delegation. But to secure effective action in such a conference, precise prior understandings between the principal powers would be necessary. To assemble an international conference without a definite program and positive agreements on major policies and objectives is a certain assurance of failure.

Thus, the debt notes from Europe presented the whole complex of world economic stabilization; for while debts were not a part of the projected economic conference, they were a very real part of world economy. No progress could be made in either direction without simultaneous solutions in the other.

In the campaign President Hoover had laid the groundwork for readjustment of the war debts, but with the firm proviso that any American concessions must be in return for positive compensations. The possible nature of such compensations had been hinted in his Cleveland address of October 15, wherein he had mentioned disarmament and monetary stabilization.

I am confident that if these policies which were proposed in building up in three directions—that is, disarmament, economic stabilization of the world, and the proposed use of these debts to secure the ends I have mentioned—are pursued, we can confidently hope to promote more rapid recovery, and we can greatly safeguard ourselves from future economic shocks.

But it was obvious, of course, that, after election, no American program touching foreign affairs could be advanced unless the President-elect gave it his firm moral and political support, and this by a strong public declaration of policy. The alternatives were clear; either joint action between President Hoover and Governor Roosevelt would give the United States a continuing international economic policy, or the debts would drift to default on December 15. The inevitable corollary of the latter alternative would be that the pressing issues of monetary stabilization and tariffs projected for the World Economic Conference would continue to fester from November until March or April.

En route from California to Washington President Hoover proposed joint action against these momentous problems. His telegram from Yuma, Ariz., took cognizance of an announcement from Albany on November 11 that Governor Roosevelt planned soon to journey to Warm Springs, Ga. Outlining the status of the war debts, the President invited Mr. Roosevelt to stop in Washington for a conference on the whole range of world economic problems. As the telegraphic exchanges of November 12-14, 1932, fully present the situation which then existed, the messages are quoted in full text:

PRESIDENT HOOVER'S MESSAGE

Yuma, Ariz.,<br>November 12, 1932.

Governor Franklin D. Roosevelt,
Albany, N. Y.

The Secretary of State has informed me that the British Ambassador, on behalf of his Government, has handed him a note stating that, "They believe that the regime of intergovernmental financial obligations as now existing must be reviewed; that they are profoundly impressed with the importance of acting quickly, and that they earnestly hope that the United States Government will see its way clear to enter into an exchange of views at the earliest possible moment."

The British Ambassador further asks for a suspension of the payments due by the British Government to our government for the period of the discussions suggested, or for any other period that may be agreed upon. This last suggestion clearly relates to the payment of $95,000,000 which will fall due on December 15, 1932. I have requested the Secretary of State to transmit to you a full copy of that note.

The Secretary of State has also just been informed that similar requests are to be made by other debtor governments, which likewise are obligated to make payments to the United States on December 15 next. One debtor

nation has defaulted on a payment due November 10, and another debtor
nation has served notice on our government of its incapacity to make a
payment due in December. Thus, our government is now confronted
with a world problem of major importance to this Nation.

The moratorium which I proposed a year ago in June—that is, the
year's postponement of intergovernmental debts and the spread of the
deferred payments over ten years—was approved by the Congress. It
served a great purpose in staying destruction in every direction and giving
to Europe a year in which to realize and so modify their attitude on solely
European questions as to support their credit structure from a great deal
of further destruction. They have made very substantial progress during
that year in financial adjustments among themselves and toward armament
reduction.

Practically all of our World War debt settlements were made, not by
the executive, but by the Commission created by act of Congress, and all
were approved in the form of legislation enacted by both Houses. A
year ago, in recommending to the Congress the ratification of the moratorium, I presented a statement of my views as to the whole of the relationship of ourselves to our debtor countries and pointed out that debts
to us bore no relationship to debts between other nations which grew out
of the war.

At the same time I recommended to the Congress that a new debt commission be created to deal with any situation that might arise owing to the
temporary incapacity of any individual debtor to meet its obligations to
our country during the period of world depression. Congress declined to
accede to this latter recommendation; it passed a joint resolution reading
in part as follows:

"It is hereby expressly declared to be against the policy of the Congress
that any of the indebtedness of foreign countries to the United States
should be in any manner cancelled or reduced; and nothing in this joint
resolution shall be construed as indicating a contrary policy or as implying
that favorable consideration will be given at any time to a change in the
policy hereby declared."

The limitation to purely temporary and individual action as to those
incapable of payment during the depression, expressed in the "communique"
referred to in the British note and in my recommendation to the Congress,
was evident in these documents. The refusal of the Congress to authorize
even the examination of this limited question, together with the above
resolution, gave notice to all debtor governments of the attitude of this
government toward either cancellation or reduction of existing obligations.
Therefore, any commitments which European governments may have made
between themselves could not be based upon any assurances of the United
States. Moreover, the tenor of negotiations asked for by the debtor governments goes beyond the terms of the Congressional resolution referred to.

I have publicly stated my position as to these questions, including that

I do not favor cancellation in any form, but that we should be receptive to proposals from our debtors of tangible compensation in other forms than direct payments, in expansion of markets for the products of our labor and our farms. And I have stated further that substantial reduction of world armament, which will relieve our own and world burdens and dangers, has a bearing upon this question.

If negotiations are to be undertaken as requested by these governments, protracted and detailed discussions would be necessary, which could not be concluded during my administration. Any negotiation of this question on the basis of the requests of these governments is limited by the resolution of the Congress. And if there is to be any change in the attitude of the Congress it will be greatly affected by the views of those Members who recognize you as their leader and who will properly desire your council and advice.

I am prepared to deal with the subject as far as it lies in the power of the Executive, but it must be our common wish to deal with this question in a constructive fashion for the common good of the country. I am loath to proceed with recommendations to the Congress until I can have an opportunity to confer with you personally at some convenient date in the near future.

There are also other important questions as to which I think an interchange of views would be in the public interest. The building up of world economic stability is, of course, of the greatest importance in the building up of our recovery. As you know, a world economic conference will be held during the course of the coming winter. Already two American experts have met with the technical experts of other governments to prepare a tentative agenda. While this conference may be begun during my administration, it is certain that it will not complete its labor until after you have assumed office.

Parallel with this, of course, is the disarmament conference, in which the United States has taken a leading part. This also has a great economic purpose as well as the advancement of world peace.

Time is of great importance in all these questions, and I understand that you are planning to come through Washington sometime during the latter part of next week, and I hope you will find it convenient to stop off long enough for me to advise with you. I should, of course, be only too glad to have you bring into this conference any of the Democratic Congressional leaders or other advisers you may wish.

HERBERT HOOVER.

Reduced to its essence, the problem presented was a choice between a vigorous policy of international cooperation in this whole complex of world economics, or a reversion to America's pre-war status of nationalistic economy and diplomatic isolation. Mr. Roosevelt, for the moment at least, chose the latter course.

## GOVERNOR ROOSEVELT'S REPLY

Albany, N. Y.
November 14, 1932.

The President,
Washington, D. C.

I appreciate your cordial telegram. On the subjects to which you refer, as in all matters relating to the welfare of the country, I am glad to cooperate in every appropriate way, subject, of course, to the requirements of my present duties as Governor of this State.

I shall be delighted to confer with you in Washington, but I have been confined to the house with a slight cold and I am, therefore, not able to suggest a definite date. I shall call you on the telephone as soon as the time of my departure for the South has been determined.

May I take the liberty of suggesting that we make this meeting wholly informal and personal. You and I can go over the entire situation.

I had already arranged to meet a number of the Democratic leaders of the present Congress late this month at Warm Springs. It will be helpful for me to have your views and all pertinent information when I meet with them. I hope that you also will see them at the earliest opportunity, because, in the last analysis, the immediate question raised by the British, French, and other notes, creates a responsibility which rests upon those now vested with executive and legislative authority.

My kindest regards,

FRANKLIN D. ROOSEVELT.

Eight days later, on November 22, Governor Roosevelt and Professor Raymond Moley conferred at the White House with President Hoover and Secretary of the Treasury Ogden L. Mills. The conference lasted one hour, and the two principals then were alone, after the departure of their advisers, for seventeen minutes longer.

It was agreed that President Hoover would recommend to a conference of Congressional leaders next morning that debt negotiations be opened; that the policy of "compensations" would be adherred to firmly by the United States; that Governor Roosevelt would enlist the support of the Democratic leaders in Congress during his Mayflower Hotel conferences that evening; that, following an outline of the American position through the press, by President Hoover next day, Governor Roosevelt would issue a statement expressing his agreement with the principles laid down in the Hoover declaration. Governor Roosevelt suggested that

Secretary Mills and Professor Moley draft the statement to be issued by himself, and asked them to meet him at the Mayflower Hotel the following morning at 9 o'clock. Governor Roosevelt declined an invitation to be present at the morrow's White House conference with the Congressional leaders.

It being still some two weeks before the scheduled assembly of Congress, President Hoover met with the leaders of both parties in both Houses on the morning of November 23, to outline the American position under his agreement with the Governor. Much to the astonishment of the President and Secretaries Stimson and Mills, the Democratic leaders expressed vigorous opposition to the resumption of debt discussions and flatly declined to cooperate in any such program.

Meanwhile, when Secretary Mills had called on Governor Roosevelt at the Mayflower at 9 o'clock, the appointed hour, he had been informed the President-elect would not have time to formulate his part of the public declaration until after he left Washington for Warm Springs.

It thus become apparent to President Hoover and his advisers that Governor Roosevelt, despite his assurances of the afternoon before, had no intention of supporting the program agreed upon. Equally evident to those who participated in the White House conferences of November 22 and 23 was the fact that Governor Roosevelt offered no alternative plan to bridge the interval until March 4. This historical fact later was revealed to the world by a remark of Governor Roosevelt in one of his informal press conferences. Questioned on the war debt exchanges, he had observed jovially, "That's not my baby."

Summarizing the White House conferences of November 22 and 23, the *Literary Digest* remarked:

In general, press onlookers see Mr. Roosevelt sidestepping the debt problem deftly and courteously along the line of his previous statement that, after all, this is a matter of primary concern to the present Executive and Congress. . . . Throughout his stay in Washington, Governor Roosevelt, always smiling and cheerful, indulging in small talk and persiflage on every opportunity, conferring more or less confidentially with practically every important Democrat in Congress, nevertheless remained tightlipped on the matter of debt policy and the Hoover dialogue.[1]

---

[1] Literary Digest, December 5, 1932, p. 7.

On the afternoon of November 23rd, President Hoover, in the full knowledge of Governor Roosevelt, issued to the press a formal statement outlining the American government's policy and program. This statement was a review of the entire debt problem, from the original war loans. It set forth again the American thesis of individual contracts with the several nations, and their separation, in fact as well as in law, from German reparations. It recalled the strong declaration of Congress in the moratorium resolution against further concessions, and urged again the creation of a new debt commission. It was proposed that this commission also be represented on the American delegations to the World Economic Conference and the General Disarmament Conference. The statement concluded on this grave and challenging note:

If our civilization is to be perpetuated, the great causes of world peace, world disarmament, and world recovery must prevail. They can not prevail until a path for their attainment is built upon honest friendship, mutual confidence, and proper cooperation among the nations.

These immense objectives, upon which the future and welfare of all mankind depend, must be ever in our thought in dealing with immediate and difficult problems. The solution of each one of these upon the basis of an understanding reached after frank and fair discussion, in and of itself strengthens the foundation of the edifice of world progress we seek to erect; whereas our failure to approach difficulties and differences among nations in such a spirit serves but to undermine constructive effort.

Peace and honest friendship with all nations have been cardinal principles by which we have ever guided our foreign relations. They are the stars by which the world must today guide its course—a world in which our country must assume its share of leadership and responsibility.

Late that afternoon, from his train near Lynchburg, Va., Governor Roosevelt issued his own statement, which clearly set forth his determination to have no part before March in the proposed international economic discussions. The complete text of Mr. Roosevelt's statement follows:

My conferences with the President and with leaders of my party have been most illuminating and useful. I wish to express my appreciation of the opportunity thus afforded me.

At this time, I wish to reaffirm my position on the questions that have been the principal subjects of our discussions.

As to the debt payments due December 15, I find no justification for modifying my statement to the President on November 14, when I pointed out that "the immediate questions raised by the British, French, and other notes, create a responsibility which rests upon those now vested with executive and legislative authority."

With regard to general policies respecting these debts, I firmly believe in the principle that an individual debtor should at all times have access to the creditor; that he should have opportunity to lay facts and representations before the creditor and that the creditor always should give courteous, sympathetic, and thoughtful consideration to such facts and representations.

This is a rule essential to the preservation of the ordinary relationships of life. It is a basic obligation of civilization. It applies to nations as well as to individuals.

The principle calls for free access by the debtor to the creditor. Each case should be considered in the light of the conditions and necessities peculiar to the case of each nation concerned.

I find myself in complete accord with four principles discussed in the conference between the President and myself yesterday and set forth in a statement which the President has issued today.

These debts were actual loans made under the distinct understanding and with the intention that they would be repaid.

In dealing with the debts, each government has been and is to be considered individually, and all dealings with each government are independent of dealings with any debtor government. In no case should we deal with the debtor governments collectively.

Debt settlements made in each case take into consideration the capacity to pay of the individual debtor nations.

The indebtedness of the various European nations to our government has no relation whatsoever to reparations payments made or owed to them.

Once these principles of the debt relationships are established and recognized, the method by which contacts between our government and the debtor nations may be provided are matters of secondary importance. My view is that the most convenient and effective contacts can be made through the existing agencies and constituted channels of diplomatic intercourse.

No action by the Congress has limited or can limit the constitutional power of the President to carry on diplomatic contacts or conversations with foreign governments. The advantage of this method of maintaining contacts with foreign governments is that any one of the debtor nations may at any time bring to the attention of the government of the United States new conditions and facts affecting any phase of its indebtedness.

It is equally true that existing debt agreements are unalterable save by Congressional action.

Since it was obvious that no arrangement negotiated by President Hoover in the remaining three months of his term could be ratified by Congress without Mr. Roosevelt's support and approval and, further, that no *modus operandi* negotiated by President Hoover could bind the new administration, it was at once apparent to the world that in this whole field of fundamental economic problems a long period of marking time was in prospect.

Over this unhappy outlook the press of the United States and the world reflected great public disappointment, as witness:

. . . It is highly unfortunate that Governor Roosevelt was unable to bring himself to meet the President half way. The refusal of the Governor to cooperate actively with Mr. Hoover, and his subsequent statement that the matter at issue was 'not his baby,' are indicative of a lack of largeness of vision more disquieting in a person about to become the Chief Executive of the Nation. . . . Mr. Roosevelt had an opportunity unique in the history of the American Presidency and he failed to grasp it. . . .— *Detroit Free Press, November 25, 1932.*

. . . It may be recalled that during the campaign there was heat and resentment in Democratic quarters when it was argued that a change of administration inevitably meant marking time for a number of months. Mr. Hoover has now done his utmost to prevent such a delay in respect to the debt issue. Mr. Roosevelt has felt unable to aid him. The delay must ensue. . . .—*New York Herald-Tribune, November 24, 1932.*

. . . The question is not so much how the debtor nations are to be approached as how Congress can best be kept informed of a series of complicated negotiations and settlements agreed upon which will stand a reasonable chance of ratification in the House and Senate. The debt funding commission in which Congressional leaders were members provided an admirable method of approach before, and a similar body created by Congress would undoubtedly offer the best approach today. In rejecting this method Governor Roosevelt obviously displayed more tact than courage. . . .—*New York Times, November 25, 1932.*

The debts may not be legally his baby until the fourth of March, but it seems to us that Mr. Roosevelt might wisely have given thought to the possibility that this baby, which is not now his, may soon develop into an unruly step-child, permanently lodged under his roof and disposed to play with matches. . . .—*Baltimore Sun, November 24, 1932.*

The first impact of all these futile exchanges, of course, was upon American business and finance. Thus, Bradstreet's weekly trade review, published December 3rd, presented this picture of nation-wide commercial stagnation as of the last week in November:

Reports to *Bradstreet's Weekly* from 55 key cities throughout the country indicate that business is at a standstill and shows little definite promise of early improvement. Confidence has been undermined by the failure of the business indices to maintain their seasonal gains, by the unsettled war debt problem, and by the coming session of Congress. . . . Reports more specifically indicate unsatisfactory or declining volume in a number of important lines of business. . . . Wholesale trade volume is slightly below last year, with prices substantially lower. Orders are small, buying extremely cautious.

CHART VI

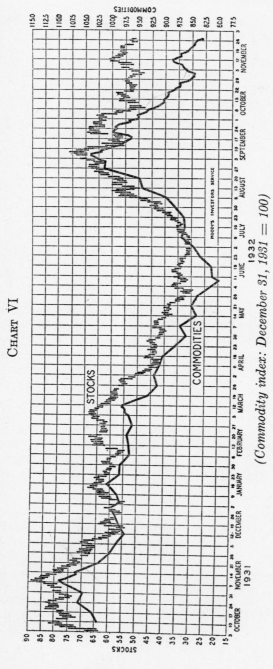

(Commodity index: December 31, 1931 = 100)

*Moody's daily index of staple commodity prices is regarded universally as the most accurate and sensitive economic index available in the United States. The above graph, as of December 1, 1932, reflects the sharp upturn in prices which followed the end of the international gold panic in June, 1932; and how all this advance of the initial recovery period was lost following the Maine elections, September 11, which accurately forecast the November triumph of New Dealism at the polls. No other country in the world suffered this reversal of the recovery tide.*

Collections are slow. Outstanding accounts of leading department stores are equal to three to four months volume of sales.

In his annual message to Congress, December 5, President Hoover re-stated his policy and program. Concerning the debts and his hopes for effective international collaboration to sustain world recovery, the President said:

Currency depreciation and correlated forces have contributed greatly to decreased price levels. Moreover, from these origins rise most of the destructive trade barriers now stifling the commerce of the world. We could, by successful action, increase security and expand trade through stability in international exchange and monetary values. By such action, world confidence could be restored. It would bring courage and stability which would reflect into every home in our land.

In response to this message, Speaker Garner announced publicly through the press what he had clearly indicated privately in the White House conference of November 23, namely, that the Democratic House of Representatives would not give even formal consideration to any proposal for recreation of the War Debt Commission.

Meanwhile, through the regular diplomatic channels, Secretary Stimson had responded to the debtors' notes, insisting upon the December 15 payments and indicating—in accordance with the White House understanding with Governor Roosevelt—that the whole question would be examined anew before the next payments became due, on June 15, 1933. As a result of much involved correspondence, $98,665,000 of the total of roundly $125,000,000 due on December 15 was paid. France, Poland, Greece, Hungary, Austria, Belgium, and Esthonia defaulted; Great Britain, Italy, Czecho-Slovakia, Latvia, Lithuania, and Finland paid in full or in part. The British payment was accompanied by a firm declaration that no further payments would be made until negotiations had been opened looking to a re-examination of the whole war debt structure.

But while diplomatic exchanges still were passing between Paris and Washington, the press carried the statement from Warm Springs that the President-elect would not insist on the December 15 payment as a condition to further negotiations. Flashed immediately to Europe by the great press associations, this statement was received with acclaim by the Paris press. At once all movement to pay the December 15 installment collapsed in France. This very casual expression of the President-elect not only cut under the official position of the United States Government in negotiations then in progress for the French payment, but pulled the ground completely from under the President and from under those groups in the French Cabinet and parliament who were working earnestly to stem the tide of repudiation sentiment in France.

On December 14 the Chamber of Deputies voted against the payment due next day.

By December 15 the world political situation again was drifting perceptibly in the direction of degeneration. Currency fluctuations were demoralizing international trade in every quarter, and the political *impasse* presented in the Hoover-Roosevelt conversations had spread profound fear throughout the business and financial capitals for the integrity of the American recovery program in the remaining days of the Seventy-second Congress. Equally shocking to American confidence, it was already a grave question among informed observers whether, as a practical matter, every claim against the war debtors had not been forfeited by the Washington government's inability to answer the British and French notes on some basis paving the way to constructive negotiations.

Worse, the confusion thrust upon world diplomacy by Governor Roosevelt's refusal to advance some workable interim plan of discussions, at once became a threat to both the disarmament conference and the projected world economic conference.

Behind the disarmament conference lay ten years' solid work by the League of Nations Preparatory Commission and months of laborious organization and discussion by the first plenary session of the conference itself.

In the still forming agenda of the economic conference lay the great hope of the world for a return to some sane basis of international financial and commercial stability. Into these conferences were thatched all that remained of the world's hopes for political stability, economic equilibrium, and lasting peace.

Unwilling to allow issues of such grave moment to stagnate or drift for three months, President Hoover, on December 17, again sought Mr. Roosevelt's cooperation in practical joint action. Under that date he telegraphed to Albany a proposal that the President-elect join with him in the selection of a special delegation of preeminently qualified men to conduct the preliminary negotiations touching the World Economic Conference, with the clear understanding (1) that war debts were not to be considered as a phase of this conference, and (2) that each debt settlement should be handled independently.

I shall be informing the Congress of the economic situation and the desirability of the above proposed machinery for dealing with these conferences, [this telegram concluded]. I should be glad to know if you could join with me in the selection of such delegation at the present time, or if you feel that the whole matter should be deferred until after March 4. I believe there would be no difficulty in agreeing upon an adequate representation for the purpose. In such selection, the first concern would be the selection of a chairman for the delegation.

At the same time President Hoover caused to be delivered to Mr. Roosevelt a draft of the special message he proposed to send to Congress during the week. The general charge to the delegation proposed would be to initiate preliminary negotiations with the British and French governments as to what program they would undertake to support in the World Economic Conference, and to determine this before any new debt settlement was discussed. Only by this procedure could the United States hope to maintain a *quid pro quo* between debt concessions and compensatory settlements in the economic conference. Should independent debt negotiations begin first, the American power to demand monetary and tariff stabilizations in the larger conference immediately would be lost. So too would be lost our influence for European disarmament.

But before any truly promising negotiations could begin in this direction two facts needed to be clearly established; first, that the proposed American delegation would speak with authority for the incoming administration, and, secondly, that the delegation should have the support of Congress. This latter condition President Hoover proposed to meet by suitable Congressional representation on the delegation.

Mr. Roosevelt replied to President Hoover's second telegram from Albany at 8:30 P.M., December 19. Again the answer was a pointed refusal to participate in joint action.

I feel that it would be both improper for me and inadvisable for you, however much I appreciate the courtesy of your suggestion, for me to take part in naming representatives. . . . I think you will recognize that it would be unwise for me to accept an apparent joint responsibility with you when, as a matter of constitutional fact, I would be wholly lacking in any attendant authority.

To such meticulous observance of the nice points of constitutional law there could be, of course, no valid objection.

Mr. Roosevelt's second refusal to joint action was received by President Hoover on the morning of December 20, the day after he had sent to Congress his special message on the whole complex of debts, disarmament, and the World Economic Conference. This message, closely following the public statement of November 23, concluded on the same note:

The situation is one of such urgency that we require national solidarity and national cooperation if we are to serve the welfare of the American people and, indeed, if we are to conquer the forces which today threaten the very foundations of civilization.

Next day President Hoover initiated a third exchange of telegrams with Governor Roosevelt. Declaring himself "unwilling to admit that cooperation cannot be established between the outgoing and incoming administrations," the President this time suggested a new plan in these words:

With a view to again making an effort to secure cooperation and that solidarity of national action which the situation needs, I would be glad if you could designate Mr. Owen D. Young, Colonel House, or any other men of your party possessed of your views and your confidence and at the same time familiar with these problems, to sit with the principal officers of this administration in endeavor to see what steps can be taken to avoid delays of precious time and inevitable losses that will ensue from such delays.

Governor Roosevelt's rejection of this proposal was telegraphed from Albany on December 21. It read in part:

The designation of a man or men of such eminence as your telegram suggests would not imply mere fact finding; it would suggest the presumption that such representatives were empowered to exchange views on matters of large and binding policy.

By way of finally washing his hands of all responsibility in the matter until March 4 Mr. Roosevelt suggested that President Hoover "proceed with the selection of your representatives to conduct the preliminary explorations necessary with individual debtor nations and representatives to discuss the agenda of the World Economic Conference, making it clear that none of these representatives is authorized to bind this government as to any ultimate policy."

This, as a practical proposition in diplomacy, amounted to the suggestion that the United States begin these delicate and complex international negotiations, which obviously would extend over four or five months, with a sixty-day policy. Its ultimate effect was to force complete abandonment of all effort in the international field until March 4.

The publication of the Hoover-Roosevelt exchanges of December 17-20 marked the end of the second phase of President Hoover's effort to secure a solid national front against Europe's concerted plan to transfer the $11,000,000,000 war debts to the backs of American taxpayers.

But the publication of these exchanges gave rise to another whirlwind of protest and condemnation of the President-elect in the press at home and abroad; and as this note was widely sustained in editorial comment for several weeks, it became apparent that Governor Roosevelt would be compelled at length to retrace his steps. This he attempted to do through an intermediary sent to Secretary Stimson's home early in January, a few days after Mr. Roosevelt had completed his term as Governor of New York. The intermediary, a mutual friend of Secretary Stimson and the Governor, represented that Mr. Roosevelt had felt deeply the criticism of the press. Accordingly, Secretary Stimson took luncheon with Governor Roosevelt on January 9, at which a second White House conference was arranged.

At this second conference, on January 20, were President Hoover, President-elect Roosevelt, Secretary Stimson, Secretary Mills, Norman Davis, the United States delegate to the disarmament conference, and Professor Moley. Mr. Roosevelt urged that a representative of Great Britain be invited to this country *soon after March 4* to discuss the debt, and that the questions concerning world economic collaboration might arise naturally in the course of such discussions. Secretary Stimson pointed out that the United States could not indicate to London that we would receive their representatives to discuss debts and then later raise all these other vital questions: that if Mr. Roosevelt intended to raise the related questions touching the World Economic Conference, the British must be so informed before sailing.

President Hoover reiterated that the need for international monetary stabilization presented a world problem of the first magnitude, and that to attempt debt negotiations first would be to sacrifice every American influence for the other great objectives of our policy, disarmament and stabilization.

After hearing some cables from Ambassador Sackett, at Berlin, the conference authorized Secretary Stimson and Professor Moley to issue an invitation to Britain to send a delegation to Washington *soon after the inauguration,* with the understanding that any discussion of debts "must be concurrent with and conditioned upon a discussion of the world's economic problems in which the two governments are mutually interested. . . ."

The British reply of January 26th accepted the invitation, but with the proviso:

It will be recognized that decisions on matters which constitute the subject of the approaching world economic conference, and which affect other states, *cannot be reached* before discussions take place at that conference between all the states represented there.

Here, the whole plan for the general economic conference crashed to the ground, for with debt negotiations resumed the United States now had nothing to offer for stabilization and disarmament.

From this point forward Governor Roosevelt set up his own relations with the British Ambassador and carried forward his discussions directly through Sir Ronald Lindsay.

Late in January, Sir Ronald made a dramatic airplane flight to Warm Springs, and then hastened back to New York to board a vessel for England. The precise nature of this important mission never has been revealed. Neither President Hoover nor Secretary Stimson was apprised officially of the ground covered between the British Ambassador and the President-elect at Warm Springs. Sir Ronald, however, considered his findings so important that he would not trust them to the telephone or cables.

Now, February 1 was at hand. The upshot of two and a half months of negotiations between the outgoing and incoming administrations was that nothing would be attempted in these pressing problems of world concern until after March 4.

Five months were lost.

The explanation of this evasion and refusal to give cooperation is today very clear. Mr. Hoover was driving hard toward world currency stabilization. Mr. Roosevelt was determined to devalue the dollar or to adopt some dollar adjustment scheme which would take America off the gold standard.

But by the end of January, 1933, questions of American policy in these vital foreign relations had become of secondary importance at home. Overshadowing now were the new tremors of shock and alarm which swept through the business and financial community as men of discernment watched the New Deal in action on the world stage. The smiling abandon with which the President-elect tossed over ten years' work on debts and disarmament was profoundly disturbing. Nor is it any challenge to Mr. Roosevelt's motives to say that his conduct in this interval left every capital bewildered and confused concerning America's future part in world organization. Hope for effective international collaboration had not been entirely shattered, but a debilitating standstill until March appeared, to many, quite as inescapable as unnecessary. And beyond March 4 lay only new stretches of uncertainty, for in all the exchanges between November 12 and January 20 there had been no hint on Mr. Roosevelt's part of a positive policy for dealing with the questions to come before the World Economic Conference.

The announcement from London, early in February, that the conference had been postponed indefinitely served only to deepen such doubts and misgivings.

As our hesitant economic confidence now slumped sharply, the forces of disintegration again took command in the United States. Save as a daring speculation, no international business or financial contract of any sort was possible. Secondly, the monetary stresses which flowed from the international *impasse* grievously aggravated political suspicions and diplomatic intrigues in both Europe and Asia.

Above all, there had arisen in this country profound fears that Mr. Roosevelt's firm stand against clearly stated economic preparations for March 4 presaged some measure of gold revalorization, currency management under the Warren theories, or outright inflation.

It was growing conviction on all these points which set in motion on an ever-widening scale, during January, 1933, the pressures of hoarding and hysteria which marked secondary phase of the national banking debacle.

At any moment in this period, Mr. Roosevelt might easily have calmed all these fears and apprehensions by a single vigorous statement pledging unequivocal support of the existing gold standard. Through his control over Congress, he might also have demanded resolutely an immediate fulfillment of his campaign pledges to a balanced federal budget.  And he might have repudiated with a single courageous declaration the whole storm of inflation chatter on Capitol Hill.  Instead he remained, to all public knowledge, aloof and unconcerned—a circumstance which, of itself, gave substance in many minds to the suspicions which lay at the heart of the gathering panic.

Suggestions that the President-elect take one or all of these steps were offered repeatedly during January by a number of influential Democratic leaders outside of Congress.  To each, Mr. Roosevelt gave the same jovial answer—that he would assume no responsibility until noon on March 4.

## Chart VII—THE CURVE OF PANIC

*Hoarded currency is a vivid index of mass moods. The follow-ing graph traces the curve of panic and tranquillity from Novem-ber, 1930, through January, 1933.*

*Observe how sharply demand for money rose following the 1930 election, and again in April, 1931, with the Austrian col-lapse; how fear was allayed by the Hoover moratorium in June; how it rose with the spread of European panic to England in August-September; how it was allayed in October by the creation of the National Credit Corporation; how it rose in December with domestic banking difficulties; how it was allayed in February, 1932, by the creation of the Reconstruction Finance Corporation and other federal measures; how it rose again in June with in-flation threats in Congress; how it was allayed in July by the adjournment of Congress and the taking hold of the forces of recovery.*

*Forces influencing this curve between the 1932 election and President Roosevelt's inauguration on March 4, 1933, are traced in succeeding chapters.*

### HOARDED CURRENCY

WEEKLY INCREASES (+) AND DECREASES (−) IN HOARDING

3 WEEKS MOVING AVERAGE

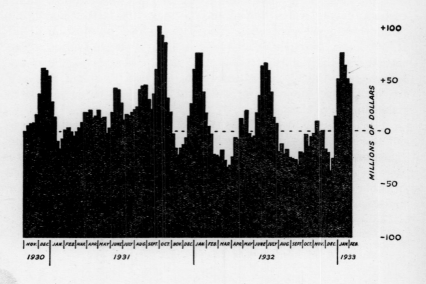

# CHAPTER IV

## THE SPEAKER SPEAKS

THE historical evidence now is clear that there was but one immediate and decisive national impulse behind the bank panic—steadily mounting fears that Mr. Roosevelt, at election day 1932, held at least an open mind on the questions of gold suspension and inflation.

But these doubts and fears of the New Deal, since so substantially vindicated, did not come upon the national mind full blown. They were first questions, then suspicions—planted in scattered seeds of equivocation, and nurtured over a period of two months (November and December, 1932) by Mr. Roosevelt's repeated evasions touching money, gold, tariffs and international economic stabilization. They burst at length in the full flower of panic, in January, when the President-elect, at his Warm Springs, Georgia, retreat began to council openly and freely with avowed advocates of gold revalorization, managed currency and free silver.[1]

Before documenting the development of this primary impulse of panic, however, (Chapter VI) we explore briefly in this chapter and the next, two subsidiary events of the post-election interregnum, events which helped set the stage by further assaulting public confidence generally. The first was the publication of all R.F.C. loans, as demanded so insistently by Speaker Garner. The second was the failure of the House of Representatives, under the leadership of the Vice-President-elect, to accept President Hoover's tax and budget program for the fiscal year 1933-34, or a budget-balancing equivalent.

The R.F.C. publicity closed several hundred banks which, without the added pressures of "publicity runs" might have weathered the storm; and the December-January failure of the House of Representatives, so quickly responsive to Mr. Roosevelt's wishes in other directions, to come to grips firmly with the problems of taxes and budget, served only to confirm in many minds, already

---

[1] During the last week of January the press associations, from Warm Springs, quoted Henry A. Wallace: "The smart thing would be to go off the gold standard a little farther than England has."

widespread fears of ultimate inflation through Federal fiscal operations.[2]

All three of these disturbing movements were operative simultaneously upon the public mind, and were mutually aggravating. But our reconstruction of the period is upon a chronological scheme. We attempt to measure the impact of each successive blow to recovery as it fell, and to trace how the whole series of events from the very outset, at election day 1932, pointed with ever-increasing clarity in one direction, namely, to gold abandonment, soft money and inflation. The first tangible evidence of this prospective policy came, as we have seen, in the White House meetings on debts and the World Economic Conference.

While business waited in vain from November until late January for a positive cue as to Mr. Roosevelt's program for international economic stabilization, a second brake upon recovery developed a devastating impact in the United States during December and early January. The publication of all Reconstruction Finance loans from month to month since late August, 1932, had precipitated a new epidemic of bank runs touching practically every state. On top of this there began to appear, at early November, new evidences of scattered regional money panics arising from inflation fears. Stated another way, the impact of prospective New Deal monetary policies fell in November upon a banking structure already shamefully weakened by the premeditated political sabotage of the R.F.C. "publicity runs."

The R.F.C. publicity amendment, passed under the personal leadership of Mr. Garner in July, had been resisted by President Hoover and every financial officer of the government. As anticipated, the measure had proved a double assault upon banking during the crucial recovery period. First, the publication of the loans threw needless alarms into hundreds of communities every thirty days. At the same time, the policy also restrained hundreds of sound banks from seeking R.F.C. assistance against such periodic neighborhood excitements. The ultimate consequence of the publicity, therefore, was to tighten credit generally, at a time when public confidence and fluid credit offered the only hope of recovery.

---

[2] At mid-January, 1933, the Federal Reserve Bank of New York circulated a confidential memorandum upon the prospective effects of devaluation.

In his man-to-man whispering campaign in the House of Representatives during June and July, 1932, Speaker Garner circulated the report that loan applications from Republicans were being given preference at the R.F.C. His campaign was centered upon a credit of $90,000,000 which had been extended to General Charles G. Dawes' bank in Chicago early in June, some sixty days after Mr. Dawes had resigned as Chairman of the R.F.C. The fact that announcement of this loan had been published by the Dawes bank in all Chicago newspapers the day it had been approved in Washington was either unknown to Speaker Garner, or was purposely ignored by him in his drive against "Wall Street's three-billion dollar soup kitchen," as he once described the R.F.C. in a conference with newspapermen.

Likewise, the Speaker neglected the fact that the Dawes loan had been approved in advance by the late Melville A. Traylor, president of the First National Bank of Chicago. At that moment Mr. Traylor was being discussed widely as a prospective presidential nominee of the Democratic party. It also had been urgently recommended by the three Democratic directors of the R.F.C., of whom Mr. Jesse Jones was on the ground at Chicago.

Ignored also was the fact that President Hoover, with a view expressly to avoiding such demagogic attack upon this vital recovery agency, had shifted the R.F.C. board from a Republican to a Democratic majority. In this shift, former Senator Atlee Pomerene, of Ohio, had been named chairman. Moreover, in February, 1932, Mr. Jesse Jones, of Texas, a lifelong friend of Mr. Garner, had been nominated an R.F.C. director on the personal insistence of the Speaker. This appointment had been Mr. Garner's price for allowing the R.F.C. bill to pass the House.

When the publicity amendment was approved by the House in July, the R.F.C. directors immediately addressed strong protests to the respective banking committees of the House and Senate. They warned that this provision, if enacted, would undo much, if not all, of the work already accomplished by the Corporation in preserving the credit structure of the nation. They pointed out with force that advances already had been made to some 3,600 banks, insurance companies, building and loan associations, and other reservoirs of savings. Adequate protection of the public interest could be assured, they suggested, by confidential reports to the appropriate committees of Congress.

As a result of these protests, the Senate modified the House language regarding publicity so as to provide for monthly reports to the Clerk of the House and the Secretary of the Senate. In the Senate debate leaders of both parties made it clear that the reports were not to be published save by the specific direction of Congress. In signing the Emergency Relief Act, on July 17, 1932, President Hoover stated: [3]

. . . . . the possible destructive effect on credit institutions by the so-called publicity clause has been neutralized by the declaration of the Senate leaders of all parties that this provision is not to be retroactive, and that the required monthly reports of future transactions are all of a confidential nature and must be so held by the clerks of the Senate and the House of Representatives, unless otherwise ordered by the Congress when in session.

This clear understanding of legislative intent appeared to offer assurance that, with Congress adjourned, there would be no damaging publicity of the emergency loans — at least not before December.

But, before leaving for his home in Texas, Speaker Garner instructed the Clerk of the House to release the first R.F.C. report to the press as soon as it reached Capitol Hill. Assuming personal responsibility for this command, the Speaker undertook to sustain the Clerk, if necessary, by an affirmative House vote when Congress assembled in December. Accordingly, the loans for the last half of July, for August, September, October, and November were published promptly, each tabulation appearing about three weeks after the end of the month.

In these lists every borrowing bank was named, with the amount of the R.F.C. credit. Each list carried approximately 500 names, in as many localities. The result, in hundreds of cases, was that when one bank in a small community had borrowed, depositors tended gradually to shift their balances to a bank which had not borrowed. Directly measurable or not, the net effect of the publicity was to focus increasing pressures upon those very spots which the whole R.F.C. arrangement had been designed to protect and bolster in the period of stress.

A few selected examples from the reports of the Comptroller

---

[3] White House press release.

of the Currency will serve to illustrate the incidence of these new pressures.

The State Bank of Stronghurst, Illinois, with deposits of $193,-000, received an R.F.C. loan of $18,000 in August. The loan was published on September 30. The bank failed on December 1.

The Reno National Bank, Reno, Nevada, with deposits of $4,390,000, received loans aggregating $795,500 in July, August, and October. The loans were published on August 23, September 30, and November 29. The bank suspended on December 9.

The Peoples State Bank of Harmony, Minnesota, with deposits of $274,000, received a loan of $22,000 in September. The credit was published on October 25. The bank closed on December 7.

Other examples of this deadly sequence of events, from the official records of the R.F.C. and the Comptroller of the Currency, follow:

TABLE II

| Name of bank | Deposits | R. F. C. loan | Date of loan | Date of publication | Date suspended |
|---|---|---|---|---|---|
| Bank of Statesboro, Georgia........ | $ 481,000 | $20,000 | Oct. | Nov. 29 | Dec. 6 |
| First State Bank, Carver, Minnesota | 201,000 | 8,500 | Sept. | Oct. 25 | Dec. 7 |
| Sturtevant State Bank, Sturtevant, Wisconsin ...................... | 78,000 | 11,000 | Oct. | Nov. 29 | Dec. 12 |
| United-Nevada Bank, Reno........ | 1,950,000 | 34,290 | Oct. | Nov. 29 | Dec. 12 |
| Texas Bank & Trust Co., Brownsville | 425,000 | 25,000 | Oct. | Nov. 29 | Dec. 14 |

In the month of December, 1932, alone, there were reported to the Comptroller of the Currency no less than fifty-two bank failures which had followed within sixty days the publication of their R.F.C. credits.

Even in the hundreds of localities where failures were avoided following publication, the release of the new hoarding pressures which flowed directly from publicity, exerted a paralyzing influence upon banking generally. The doubts and misgivings thus spread in several hundred communities every month constituted new demands for extreme liquidity in even the soundest banks.

With the return of Congress in December, 1932, Speaker Garner, now the Vice-President-elect, renewed his publicity drive with yet more reckless enthusiasm. He now sponsored a resolution in the House demanding publication of all R.F.C. loans of the period February-July, 1932, that is, to bring out all loans not covered by the previous publicity resolution.

Chairman Pomerene strongly urged upon the Speaker the

dangers of this course, but Mr. Garner insisted he intended to "expose" R.F.C. operations regardless of consequences. The resolution demanding publication of the earlier loans [4] was duly passed early in January, 1933. And on January 25, the complete tabulation of loans, from the launching of R.F.C. in February, 1932 to July 21, were released to the press from the Capitol office of the Speaker. This act coincided, as it happened, with conclusive news of Mr. Roosevelt's intentions concerning "reflation." (Chapter VI.)

The result was electric. Several thousand banks which had borrowed prior to July, 1932, were exposed simultaneously in late January, 1933, to all the excited pressures generated by the previous monthly lists. The fact that some of these banks had already repaid as much as 90 per cent of their loans did not exempt them from the retroactive publicity.

Where these new and wholly unnecessary pressures coincided with otherwise weakened conditions—as in Michigan—the result was immediate disaster.

Although there were many other factors in the Michigan situation,[5] where a state bank holiday was proclaimed on February 14, the publication of the R.F.C. loans on January 25—which disclosed large loans to the Detroit Guardian group as well as to other important banks throughout the state—was unmistakably an aggravating and complicating factor in the secondary phase of the national conflagration.

Publicity alone could not have precipitated the general suspension. Fear for Mr. Roosevelt's inflation policies was the heart of the difficulty. But the R.F.C. loan publicity unleashed the final pressures which exposed to full public view the real state of alarm in the banking community throughout the nation.

Even here, President Hoover still was hopeful that Mr. Roosevelt would see fit to offer some assurance on the question of money. He determined, therefore, to hold the situation from day to day, even from hour to hour, by every means at his command.

In an attempt to check the impact of the retroactive R.F.C. publicity, the President issued a statement late in January commending borrowing insitutions for their cooperation in the govern-

---

[4] H.R. 335, Seventy-second Congress, second session.
[5] The Michigan suspension is developed more fully in Chapters VII and VIII.

ment program. But as the R.F.C. loans, in many cases, had enabled the borrowing banks to withstand panic runs during the February-July crisis of 1932, the publication of the loans, in January, 1933, served only to arouse again the old impulses of local alarm. A bank "rumor" revived after one run always is more volatile than the original. Thus, with money tinkering clearly in prospect after March 4, practically all the ground gained by ten months of R.F.C. operations was lost in about ten days in January, 1933.

These results are reflected clearly in banking statistics. Bank suspensions, which had averaged 23 per week in October, 22 per week in November, and 34 in December, leaped to 54 per week for January.

Deposits resumed had exceeded deposits suspended for the four months July to October, 1932, inclusive, by an average of approximately $8,000,000 per month; but in November the excess of suspended deposits was $30,832,000. In December, net excess of suspended deposits increased to $63,580,000, and for January, 1933, bank failures leaped to 241 (the largest monthly total since January, 1932), with a net balance of suspended deposits aggregating $120,547,000. This was the largest total reported for a single month since the trough of the depression in June, 1932.

When bank failures began to be reported at the rate of ten a day during late January and the first week of February, Senators Byrnes and Robinson, after conferences with several of their Democratic colleagues, wirelessed President-elect Roosevelt aboard the Astor yacht *Nourmahal,* urging his aid in securing repeal of the Garner publicity laws. On February 2, Senator Robinson introduced a repealer in the Senate and took occasion to speak vehemently against the whole strategy of the publicity campaign since July 1932. This move was quickly abandoned by the Democratic leaders in the Senate, however, when word was flashed back from the *Nourmahal* that Mr. Roosevelt would not lend his influence to reverse Speaker Garner's policy.

Meanwhile, Mr. Robert V. Fleming, President of the Riggs National Bank of Washington, and Chairman of the Federal Legislative Committee of the American Bankers Association, again had urged Senators Byrnes and Robinson to repeal the publicity requirements. At Mr. Fleming's behest, Senator Robinson discussed the matter with the Speaker. But Mr. Garner stood his ground. Representative Bertrand H. Snell, the Republican Leader in the House, also urged Mr. Garner to abandon his personal war on the R.F.C., but without avail. When, in the same week, William Green, President of the American Federation of Labor, made a spirited personal appeal to Mr. Garner, the Speaker inquired, "Bill, why are you down here fighting the battle of the bankers?"

A few days after this interview, Mr. Charles S. McCain, a prominent New York banker who had been a Roosevelt supporter in the presidential campaign, vigorously urged repeal of the publicity laws upon Senator Robinson. On February 18, Mr. McCain conferred with Mr. Roosevelt in his New York town house. He revealed later to intimates in New York that on this occasion the President-elect again had indicated his resolute opposition to the Robinson repealer.

Before this time, however, the dangers of the whole national situation had been intensified greatly by the Michigan holiday proclamation of February 14. There was now a threat of imminent national disaster. Michigan was a fire which must be checked at once.

Despite his private knowledge that Mr. Roosevelt favored retention of the publicity amendments, President Hoover, on February 20, again urged Congress to repeal the destructive Garner provisions.

I earnestly recommend repeal of the procedure of the House of Representatives in publishing loans made by the R. F. C. These transactions should be open to the fullest degree to the Representatives of Congress, but their publication in the last few months has led to widespread misinterpretation, mostly innocent but vicious in effect, by depositors and alarmists who do not recognize that such borrowings represent an endeavor of the institutions to provide funds needed in service of their respective communities. This publication is destroying the usefulness and effectiveness of the Reconstruction Finance Corporation, is exaggerating fears, and is introducing a new element of grave danger. It is drying up the very sources of credit. The effect of such publication is forcing payment by distressed debtors to replenish bank funds. It is causing hoarding of currency.

This was indeed a temperate statement of the situation which then existed. But current figures on bank failures are not ordinarily available to the public. And the President could not make them public at the White House in support of his message to Congress without pouring oil upon the prairie fire of panic. Michigan was in flames, so to speak, and already Ohio and Indiana were exhibiting secondary tremors of the same general excitements. Neither could the President reveal the alarming repercussions of these scattered regional panics upon the Federal Reserve Bank at Chicago. Only the Treasury, the Federal Reserve Board, the R.F.C., and the White House could see from hour to hour the destructive forces at work on the national credit structure. In Washington there were genuine alarms, that unless the services of the R.F.C. could be re-established within 72 hours the Michigan disturbance would engulf the nation. But Congress, informed of Mr. Roosevelt's view of the matter, declined to act.

On March 14, 1933, a few days after his resignation from the R.F.C., Chairman Pomerene was interviewed at Cleveland on the subject of this R.F.C. publicity.

"It was the most damnable and vicious thing that was ever done," he told an Associated Press correspondent. "It almost counteracted all the good work we had been able to do."

This interview continued:

The banks which got R. F. C. loans were good banks. The loans were amply secured, as the law required. Requests for loans did not mean that applicant banks were unsound, but some silly persons construed them that way.[6]

An equally vehement Democratic protest against R.F.C. loan publicity came three weeks later from Governor A. Harry Moore, of New Jersey—almost a month *after* the national banking resumption. In a letter to Senator Warren W. Barbour, of New Jersey, dated April 5, 1933, Governor Moore said: [7]

The last publications of Reconstruction Finance Corporation loans to banks did incalculable harm. To continue these publications will mean further runs on banks and ruin to many. Again, I vehemently repeat my protest as Governor of New Jersey to the publication of names of banks. Such publication can serve no good purpose and only serves to undo the good work which the President has accomplished in restoring confidence. Senator Robinson deserves support and cooperation in his effort to remedy this situation.

This letter is but representative of hundreds received by mem-

---

[6] Washington Star, March 14, 1933.
[7] Congressional Record, Seventy-third Congress, 1st session, p. 1303, temporary binding.

bers of the House and Senate during the period August, 1932-
March, 1933.   Many were read into the *Congressional Record* from
day to day.   All testify to the deliberate sabotage of the R.F.C.
program by the violent partisanship of the Speaker of the House
of Representatives.   They testify, too, that from day to day Mr.
Garner must have been fully informed as to the disastrous consequences of his policy.

Nor may it be said in his defense that he acted upon a deep conviction of public policy demanding full publicity for all transactions in governmental finance; for when legislation was proposed in
January, 1934, to set up the $2,000,000,000 exchange-stabilization
fund, subject to secret control by the President and the Secretary
of the Treasury, the Vice-President declined to lend his influence
to a group of Senators who sponsored an amendment to require a
*secret* monthly report to Congress on the stabilization operations.

Eloquent to the same point is the fact that in the further amendment of the R.F.C. act in the special session of the Seventy-third
Congress, in May, 1933, the Garner publicity provision was quietly
repealed by solid Democratic majorities in both Houses.

But its deadly work had been done.

CHAPTER V

## CONGRESS AND THE BUDGET

CONCURRENTLY with the breakdown of all international stabilization efforts and the release of new domestic banking pressures through inflation fears coincident with the R.F.C. publicity, American business confidence was further assaulted in the post-election interregnum by the failure of the hold-over Congress to adopt a sound fiscal program directed to an honestly-balanced federal budget.

When Congress assembled on December 5, 1932, government finances were in a precarious state. Although a "billion-dollar tax bill" acceptable to the Democratic House finally had been passed in June, Treasury collections during the summer and fall had revealed many phantom revenues in the law. The taxes imposed simply did not yield the revenues estimated by the House and Senate committees.

The first session of the Seventy-second Congress (December, 1931-July, 1932) had torn President Hoover's budget-balancing tax program to shreds, and then imposed prodigious new spending under the Wagner-Garner emergency relief bill. As a result, the gross national debt had increased during the calendar year 1932 by roundly $3,000,000,000, slightly more than half of which, however, was represented by R.F.C. loans. Moreover, since July 1, 1931, when the depression inroads on profits and income began to be reflected in tax receipts, the national debt had increased, up to December 1, 1932, by no less than $4,640,000,000.

The bitter experience of every nation in Europe in the period of post-war financial reorganization stood as clear warning to the United States that there could be no sound progress toward economic recovery until a balanced budget had been achieved. Government credit is the keystone of all credit. Industry cannot move forward so long as huge government loans are bleeding the investment market. Worse, heavy government borrowing, if long continued solely for budgetary management, leads inexorably to inflation of the currency; and this threat intimidates all investment confidence so long as governmental finances are seriously out of balance. Business stagnation is the inevitable consequence of recurrent national deficits. No nation ever has escaped this penalty.

But there was a great element of hope in our position as the Seventy-second Congress assembled for its second session in December, 1932. The unequivocal pledges of both parties in the campaign apparently had aroused Congress thoroughly to the urgency of sound fiscal policies.[1] As the session began there was a widespread assumption that, with politics presumably adjourned following the election, the outgoing administration and the expiring Congress would move resolutely to a solid budgetary program. At best, budget curtailment and higher taxes always are painful ventures to members of Congress. But no occasion offers a more favorable opportunity for these ends than the last session of a Congress coincident with the expiration of an Administration willing to assume political responsibility for new taxes. Such was the rare opportunity presented in this last "Lame Duck" session.

Paring departmental estimates by $830,000,000 under the then current appropriations, and then adding $250,000,000 for anticipated relief and emergency expenditures, President Hoover, on December 6, 1932, submitted a budget[2] which called for net reductions of $580,000,000 in federal expenditures. On the side of revenues the President recommended a general manufacturers' excise tax of 2¼ per cent, to yield approximately $350,000,000 a year in additional income, plus a one-year extension of the federal gasoline tax, to yield about $137,000,000. With these and certain minor adjustments the outlook for the 1933 fiscal year was:

| | |
|---|---|
| Expenditures | $3,250,000,000 [3] |
| Revenues | 2,950,000,000 |
| Deficit | $ 300,000,000 |

On the revenue side of this calculation, however, was an item of approximately $250,000,000 due on the war debt payments from Europe, which almost certainly would be postponed. The actual prospective deficit for the fiscal year 1934, therefore, stood at

[1] In his campaign address at Pittsburgh, Pa., October 19, 1932, Mr. Roosevelt had said: "I regard reduction in Federal spending as one of the most important issues of this campaign. In my opinion it is the most direct and effective contribution that government can make to business."
[2] For the fiscal year beginning July 1, 1933.
[3] Exclusive of $498,000,000 sinking fund requirements.

roundly $550,000,000. But under continued business recovery this deficit might easily have been financed by repayments to the R.F.C., with the result that new government borrowing would dwindle after January, 1933, and stop entirely not later than June.

As a further check upon federal spending, President Hoover submitted for Congressional approval early in December a series of 58 executive orders consolidating and regrouping administrative divisions and bureaus, in the interest of economy and efficiency. Because this reorganization program had not been worked out as to details of personnel, the budget calculations did not take account of the additional economies anticipated from this source. But they were recognized as a considerable item, running perhaps $25,000,000 a year.

In presenting his budget recommendations, the President vigorously urged this program, or the equivalent, as "the foundation of economic recovery."

"Such a situation can not be continued without disaster to the federal finances," he said in reviewing the accumulating deficits since 1931. His message concluded on the note:

I can not too strongly urge that every effort be made to limit expenditures and avoid additional obligations, not only in the interest of the already heavily burdened taxpayer, but in the interest of the very integrity of the finances of the Federal Government.

In view of the campaign pledges of both parties there could be, of course, no public opposition to this demand for a balanced budget. Mr. Roosevelt, in his Pittsburgh address on October 19, had personally pledged a reduction of at least a *billion* dollars a year in federal expenditures. The Hoover program contemplated reductions of only half that amount. Repeatedly during the campaign Mr. Roosevelt had read to his audience that portion of the Democratic platform promising an "immediate and drastic reduction in governmental expenditures" all along the line, "to accomplish a saving of not less than 25 per cent in the cost of the Federal Government." He likewise had alluded repeatedly to that section of the Chicago platform pledging "maintenance of the national credit by a federal budget annually balanced on the basis of accurate executive estimates within revenues." In his radio address from Albany on July 30 interpreting the platform Mr. Roosevelt had discussed budgetary policy ahead of every other national problem:

> With these declarations—for a balanced budget and a sound currency—the Democratic party sets its face against the time-serving and disastrous fiscal policy of recent years. . . . When the depression began, the Administration, instead of reducing annual expenses to meet decreasing revenues, became sponsor for deficits which at the end of this fiscal year [1933] will have added five billion dollars to the national debt. To meet this staggering deficit, the Administration has resorted to the type of inflation which has weakened public confidence in our government both at home and abroad.
>
> High-sounding newly-invented phrases can not sugar-coat the pill.
>
> Let us have the courage to stop borrowing to meet increasing deficits. Stop the deficits! Let us have equal courage to reverse the policy of the Republican leaders and insist on a sound currency. . . . Something more is needed than a domestic balanced budget and a just revenue system. Muddled government finances create a general uncertainty concerning the value of national currencies; this uncertainty has a way of spreading from country to country. The world is tormented with it now.

In view of these clear party commitments by the President-elect, the Democratic leaders in the House and Senate could not fail to voice hearty approval of President Hoover's budget program. Daily during the week of December 6 the press of the nation fairly glowed with cordial lip service to courageous statesmanship. On Capitol Hill, for a time, leaders crowded each other in a wordy scramble toward a balanced budget. Speaker Garner and the late Democratic Floor Leader, Mr. Henry T. Rainey, were conspicuous among those who, in newspaper statements, publicly endorsed the principle. Since, under the Constitution, the revenue measures necessarily would originate in the House, where these gentlemen were in absolute control, their public approval of the Hoover program was, for that week, doubly reassuring to the country.

Unfortunately, however, all this great enthusiasm for economy and taxes was limited to press releases. Nothing happened. The House Ways and Means Committee did not even assemble to consider a tax bill until early January. The three weeks preceding the Christmas holiday passed without final legislative action on a single bill of primary domestic concern, save a measure to grant independence to the Philippine Islands—which was vetoed.

As a matter of fact, the enactments of December, 1932, comprised a number of private pension bills, several measures establishing new bird sanctuaries, some rearrangements of national park boundaries, and half a dozen bills relating to streets and alleys, barber regulations, and traffic rules in the District of Columbia.

From this historic session of Congress the first legislation to reach President Hoover for his signature, in December, was a measure "for the relief of John S. Shaw." It was a routine pension bill, one of hundreds which pass every session.

Next came a bill authorizing the Secretary of the Treasury to pay employees of the House and Senate their December salaries on the twentieth of the month, instead of the thirtieth, so no one would be short of Santa Claus money.

On December 19 a monumental measure was passed to provide for the "restitution of certain postoffice employees at Detroit, Michigan."

On the same day President Hoover signed a measure authorizing the Commissioners of the District of Columbia to close certain streets and alleys rendered useless by the march of time.

On December 23 a bill extending the privileges of "Congressional" auto license plates to certain employees of the Capitol became the law of the land. Another measure signed that day required all barber shops in the District of Columbia to close one day a week. A third bill the same day authorized the transfer of Widows Island, Maine, by the Secretary of the Navy to the jurisdiction of the Department of Agriculture for a migratory bird refuge.

These vital measures of the second Garner session complete the legislation enacted in 1932. But on January 3 Congress promptly resumed the ponderous production of chicken-feed. It completed action that day on a bill authorizing the Secretary of the Navy to sell obsolete and surplus clothing for what it might bring, without regard to the usual requirements for competitive bidding. Under the same date it extended from December 30, 1932, until March 3, 1933, the statutory reporting date of the special joint committee investigating veteran costs.

This informal "stand-still agreement" on Capitol Hill was immediately recognized by President Hoover and his legislative leaders in December, as evidence of a clear House policy of polite and bowing obstruction to the Hoover budget program. The President asked Secretary Mills, therefore, on December 18, to undertake personal negotiations with influential Democratic leaders in Congress looking to some agreement on fiscal measures. After several days of arduous negotiation, Secretary Mills reported he had obtained the pledge of Speaker Garner and his colleagues to throw in a sufficient bloc of Democratic votes to pass the sales tax, the keystone of the budget program. When word of this agreement percolated to the press gallery, Speaker Garner discreetly confirmed his pledge, and next morning, December 27, the press blazoned the glad tidings that the way had been cleared in Washington for a balanced budget!

But that afternoon the newspapers carried the "background" statement from Albany that Governor Roosevelt was "amazed" and "horrified" by the news of Speaker Garner's agreement with Secretary Mills. The plan collapsed instantly, never to be revived. It was at this juncture that Chairman Collier of the House Ways and Means Committee announced that hearings on the tax program would begin on January 3. One precious month already was lost, and only two months remained before inauguration—a very short time indeed for enactment of a general tax bill.

Although Governor Roosevelt's rejection of the Garner-Mills agreement left Capitol Hill in a state of shocked bewilderment and confusion, with Congressmen openly asking whither they now might turn for leadership, the incident revealed to the country at large a controlling situation which had been realized in official Washington since mid-November, namely, that the President-elect had determined to exercise secretly his party leadership in the Hoover short session.

True, Mr. Roosevelt had declared publicly in the debt negotiations his policy of complete aloofness until March 4; yet it had been common knowledge in the Capitol corridors since the White House meeting of November 22, that Senator James F. Byrnes, of South Carolina, had been designated as Mr. Roosevelt's personal spokesman on legislative policies. Through this private channel had come the declaration on November 29 that no Presidential appointments were to be confirmed in the "Lame Duck" session. Early in December had come the informal signal for the passage of the domestic allotment farm relief plan before March 4. Now, late in December came the direct word of the President-elect's repudiation of Mr. Garner's parliamentary agreement on the tax program. Despite the assertion in his telegram of November 14 that war debts presented "a responsibility which rests upon those now vested with executive and legislative authority," there no longer could be any doubt in President Hoover's mind that Mr. Roosevelt had determined to assume control and direction of the Congressional session. Through the Democratic majority in the House, it was easily within Mr. Roosevelt's power quietly to wave "stop" or "go" on every measure before the session. But because this whole system of contact and direction was shrouded in the deepest secrecy of personal confidences, the actions and decisions of the President-elect were, for the moment, wholly free of any burden of public responsibility or personal accountability.

By the well-established traditions of constitutional procedure, the position of the President-elect between November and March had become clearly defined in American politics. The normal course was for the incoming President to hold himself entirely aloof from Congress. In several historic cases there had been active cooperation between the outgoing and incoming administrations, on the basis of clearly stated policies and programs. But Mr. Roosevelt adopted the unprecedented course of privately exercising his tremendous political influence upon Congress while repeatedly proclaiming aloofness from all legislative proceedings.

Even where the positive Roosevelt policies were embodied in legislation, as in the Jones Domestic Allotment Bill in the House, the President-elect did not at the outset publicly announce his program. His plan of theoretical aloofness, concurrent with practical political interference through private contacts, precipitated and sustained utter confusion in legislative affairs during the entire session. At a time when issues of the gravest moment pressed for decision, Mr. Roosevelt's plan left the constitutional President without a practical working arrangement in Congress; and where the real political authority lay, rested no official responsibility, no program, no disposition to that degree of cooperation which might have solved the dilemma. The result, of course, was a Roman Holiday of utterly demoralizing partisan obstruction in the House. Mr. Roosevelt would not permit enactment of President Hoover's program. Nor did he offer an alternative program to catch the now visibly faltering confidence of the nation.

At about this juncture, late December 1932, another distracting blow to national confidence fell without warning. From the halls of Columbia University, the Technocracy group had been rending the air for some two months with new hallucinations of "revolution." By Christmas, Technocracy had become a national frenzy. Then, on December 28, Colonel E. M. House, an intimate political adviser of the President-elect, appeared in *Liberty* with a survey of current affairs styled, *"Does America Need a Dictator?"* His article, which was widely reprinted in the newspapers, warned that unless conditions changed quickly for the better "we are almost certain to have trouble."

"While the revolutionary leader is not in sight at the moment, he might appear over night."

And in conclusion, Colonel House offered this thought to the jittery nation:

The pillars of faith are shattered and there is but little left to uphold the temple in which our capitalistic civilization is sheltered.

Concurrently, from the Tabernacle of the Little Flower in Detroit, the Reverend Charles E. Coughlin was broadcasting inflammatory tidings of revolution every Tuesday and Friday over nation-wide radio chains. From New York, the Committee For the Nation, a New Deal subsidiary, was flooding the newspapers of the country with the monetary panaceas of Professor George F. Warren, now an acknowledged adviser of the President-elect on gold and currency.

But in Congress the mills of the demagogues continued to grind exceedingly fine. On December 28 the word came from Albany that President Hoover's 58 executive orders reorganizing the federal establishment should be vetoed by the House, and three weeks later, on January 19, this program, which embodied the essence of 25 years' effort toward modernization of our ponderous and costly Washington bureaucracy, was rejected by the House without even the formality of committee hearings.

Meanwhile, however, there had been a sweeping adverse editorial reaction throughout the country to the celebrated "horrified" statement of the President-elect. In an effort to recoup the situation, Governor Roosevelt invited the Democratic Congressional leaders to his New York City residence for a legislative conference on January 5, 1933. Here, the President-elect privately reaffirmed his rejection of the Garner-Mills tax agreement, and proposed higher income taxes all along the line as a means to the needed new revenues. He told the Congressional leaders he opposed a sales tax because any levy upon basic necessities fell as a "cruel" burden upon the poor—this despite the fact that at the moment his lieutenants in the House were resolutely advancing the domestic allotment farm plan, which contemplated a processing tax of nearly 100 per cent on wheat and approximately 70 per cent on cotton. In the proposed Hoover tax program the staple foods and clothing had been exempted.

Publication of the projected Roosevelt income levies, a few days later, unleashed a second whirlwind of indignant editorial protest. Alfred E. Smith summarized the revenue outlook at this point with the characteristic observation, "As far as I can see, twice nothing still leaves nothing." Before the week was out, the Democratic leaders in the House and Senate had publicly repudiated their own alternative program of taxation!

During the ten days following this national exposure of utterly leaderless confusion in Congress, which coincided with the beginning of Mr. Roosevelt's private discussion of "managed currency," there occurred incipient banking panics in Cleveland, Chattanooga, Little Rock, Mobile, St. Louis, and Memphis. The country was on exceedingly thin ice. It needed positive assurances that sound money would be maintained by the incoming administration. It needed assurance of a balanced budget, as a further safeguard against the inflationary tendencies now so plainly visible in Mr. Roosevelt's actions. Finally, it needed an immediate end of R.F.C. loan publicity.

In another desperate effort to bring order out of the legislative paralysis, President Hoover sent a vigorous special message to Congress on January 17, warning of the rapidly disintegrating economic situation, and again urging prompt enactment of the sales tax as the only practical method of balancing the budget.

I regret to say that the same forces are at work which threatened the savings of several hundreds of millions which we sought to effect at the

last session of Congress. We, during the current year, have been suffering
from that failure. . . . Every principle of sound governmental management and wise economic policy calls for the prompt balancing of the
federal budget.

Three days later the House Ways and Means Committee, by a
formal record vote, definitely rejected the sales tax program. In
lieu, "a broad survey" in quest of new sources of revenue was
announced. With but five weeks of the short session remaining,
this move clearly indicated there would be no real revenue bill
before March 4.

The same political sabotage awaited the Hoover recommendations for federal economies. The first appropriation bill passed by
the session, the First Deficiency Act, was not completed until
January 20, 1933, eight weeks after Congress assembled. It was
vetoed promptly by the President because of its provision to require
Congressional approval of all tax refunds in excess of $20,000. The
purely political character of this amendment, which had been
sponsored by Senator Kenneth D. McKellar of Tennessee, is evinced
by the fact that the proposal was not enacted in the two succeeding
sessions of the Seventy-third Congress. But it served well as an
effective obstruction to legislation in the prelude to panic.

One after another, the nine departmental appropriation bills
were piled up in the Senate, to be sent to the White House in a
heap during the last three weeks of the session. The Hoover
economies were uniformly rejected. But some compensatory "savings" were realized in committee by the bald elimination of expenditures which necessarily would be restored in later deficiency
appropriations. Several appropriation bills were passed with considerable increases over the budget estimates, without a thought
how the necessary revenues might be raised. The orgy ended in
March with the District of Columbia appropriations bill (to oper-
ate the city of Washington) lost in the adjournment jam. The
billion-dollar Independent Offices bill, which carried funds for some
56 administrative bureaus and commissions, was vetoed because it
carried $130,000,000 more than Mr. Hoover's budget estimates.
The final tabulations of the session showed an aggregate of $161,-
000,000 in appropriations over and above the budget estimates,
with the District of Columbia bill still to come with approximately

$45,000,000 more. A year after these events, the New York Times *Yearbook* for 1933 aptly characterized the session on budget policy with the observation: "Both Houses of Congress proceeded in a lackadaisical fashion, making practically no effort to reduce expenditures."

Such was the balanced budget—"the foundation of economic recovery"—as affected by Governor Roosevelt's secret command in Congress between December 1932 and March 1933.

Ten days after his inauguration, President Roosevelt sent to Congress his now historic "economy message." Here, he frankly acknowledged the influence of budgetary deficits as a direct cause of the national banking panic. He said in part:

For three long years the Federal Government has been on the road to bankruptcy. I point out to the Congress the profound effect of this fact upon our national economy. It has contributed to the recent collapse of our banking structure. It has accentuated the stagnation of the economic life of our people. It has added to the ranks of the unemployed.

But these self-evident truths of March had been, in December, January, and February, merely the obsessions of "the budget-balancing school."

CHART VIII

## INDUSTRIAL PRODUCTION: UNITED STATES AND
## WORLD EXCLUDING UNITED STATES

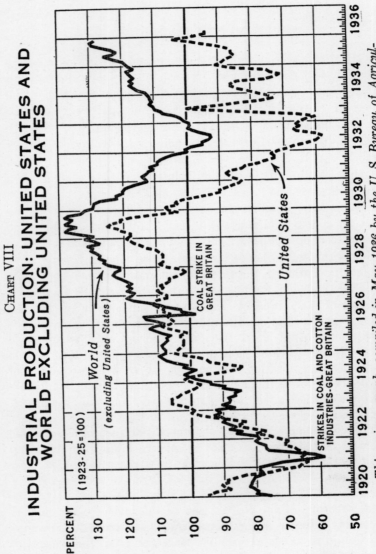

*This unique graph, compiled in May 1936 by the U.S. Bureau of Agriculture Economics, shows an almost perfect synchronization between American and world industrial production until the last quarter of 1932. From that point, the United States' index fell back sharply to the trough of July 1932.*

# CHAPTER VI

## SOFT MONEY EMERGES

IN THE light of the foregoing résumé of the initial recovery period it will not be difficult for the reader now to throw his mind back for a moment to the posture of affairs at the presidential elections of November 1932. Some four months previously, the world tide had turned definitely from depression, but with the triumph of the New Deal at the polls, our domestic recovery faltered.

At this juncture the American economic structure stood as a figurative three-legged stool. The immediate prospect of international monetary stabilization was the first leg of our hopes, for without an end to gold warfare in world trade there could be no sustained economic improvement. An honestly balanced federal budget was the second leg of the stool, for so long as huge government deficits continued, the threat of ultimate inflation hung ominously over the land. Because of the generally recognized inflationist support of the successful Democratic candidates in the election campaign, unequivocal assurance of sound money at home was the third vital need of the hour. Obviously recovery could be advanced only by all three of these policies. No two legs could long sustain our economic organization. It was the successive destruction of each of these three fundamental supports to public confidence which plunged the United States into the cruel and wholly unnecessary distress of the general banking moratorium.

We have examined in detail the "good politics" which dictated the refusal of the President-elect to involve himself in the problems of world monetary stabilization. In the shocking collapse of the London Economic Conference of 1933 the reasons for Mr. Roosevelt's 1932 policy appeared clearly. We next traced the political sabotage of the R.F.C., and of the budget-balancing tax and economy program in the "Lame Duck" session of the Seventy-second Congress. Federal spending since has given the reason for this latter policy in 1932. We turn now to the then obscure events in New York City, Albany, and Warm Springs, Georgia, which

67

gradually informed the whole world, in January 1933, of Mr. Roosevelt's predeliction to soft money.

Precisely when the President-elect began to discuss gold abandonment and managed currency as a prospective positive policy among that "most intimate circle of tight-lipped friends"[1] is not yet definitely established in the public record. It is certain, however, that as early as December 18, 1932, he conferred on the subject at Albany with a group of political advisers, among whom was a government official of high responsibility in banking. Two days later, substantial rumors of this conference were confirmed at the Treasury in Washington. The reports then confirmed, informally, had reached the Treasury from New York City. Without official knowledge of their original source in New York, Treasury officials were able to connect them indirectly with the name of Professor Raymond Moley. This story, however, did not reach the press at the time.

Despite the unqualified pledge in the Democratic national platform to "a sound currency to be maintained at all hazards," and Mr. Roosevelt's several campaign affirmations of that plank, it became clear as soon as he began his Warm Springs conferences, about mid-January, that the President-elect was counselling freely with the advocates of every form of inflation.

There appeared for a short time a somewhat general disposition among business men to dismiss these conversations as mere gestures to the political trumpeting of the inflationists. But it was not many days before penetrating observers realized that the threat of currency tinkering was very real. To those who could read between the lines, the news despatches from Georgia carried strong intimations that Mr. Roosevelt privately was encouraging the money doctors, if not by frank endorsement of their panaceas, at least by offering friendly ear to every monetary hallucination recorded in the history of man.

During the last half of January the banking and financial community fairly sizzled with rumors from Warm Springs that soft money of some sort must be expected in the new administration. Wall Street operators who were widely recognized as political intimates of Mr. Roosevelt whispered to their business associates

---

[1] Ernest K. Lindley, *The Roosevelt Revolution*, p. 64.

that dollar revalorization was much in the air. To many who enjoyed the confidence of the President-elect, advance knowledge of this policy offered the prospect of fabulous speculative profits.

The mere suggestion that such a policy was in contemplation, of course, was a destructive impulse to gold hoarding and metallic export. Moreover, it was intimated broadly in the public actions of Mr. Roosevelt himself on several occasions, that the monetary theories of Professors George F. Warren and James Rogers, two of America's most conspicuous advocates of managed currency, were the starting point of the Warm Springs discussions.

As all these rumors and suspicious were flashed around the country on private wires and by telephone, intense new waves of uncertainty and hesitation swept the banking world. The result was an insensate rush for bank liquidity. So alarming did this tendency become during the third week in January that Secretary of the Treasury Mills felt called upon to publish, through the North American Newspaper Alliance, a long and vigorous statement tracing the consequences of inflation in Europe after the war, and warning America that such steps must not be seriously considered. This statement, designed to check inflation sentiment in Congress and to reassure American bank depositors, was published in the principal newspapers of the United States on January 23 and 24.

When people learn that money is to be devalued, or shifted from gold to a commodity-index standard, they are immediately seized by fears as to future values in general. Their first impulse is to hoard gold or buy foreign exchange in some money of a fixed standard. The man, for example, who bought $1,000,000 worth of Sterling exchange in February 1933, was able to translate his money back into about $1,500,000 ten months later. Thus, even a rumor of revalorization incites an immediate flight from the currency.

Next, bankers begin at once to strengthen their reserves against prospective deposit withdrawals. This they accomplish by calling loans and refusing all new credits.

Inevitably, therefore, a money and banking panic is absolutely certain if people have advance notice, or even well-grounded suspicions, that monetary devaluation is impending. Every currency shift in Europe since the war had demonstrated the inexorable disastrous impact of these panic pressures, and the memory of the European disasters still was fresh in the minds of the American financial community in January 1933.

But still the tide of managed-currency talk rolled on. Encouraged by the tenor of Mr. Roosevelt's private conversations—many of which were flashed instantly to the Democratic Congressional leaders in Washington—the inflation bloc on Capitol Hill took new life and began to press for immediate legislative action on their various fiat-money measures. Under the leadership of Representatives Busby of Mississippi and Goldsborough of Maryland, the Democratic majority in the House organized an informal "reflation" bloc. The publicity incident to these parliamentary maneuvers projected to the entire country the fears which theretofore had ruled only in a relatively small circle of bankers and Washington officials. The public at large recognized instantly, of course, that all this soft-money chatter in Congress might have been stopped overnight by a single firm word of repudiation from the President-elect. Instead of discouraging such excitements, however, Mr. Roosevelt gave them the tacit approval of studied silence. Gradually by these processes, the threat of managed currency became real to the entire country.

On January 28, authoritative word reached Democratic leaders on Capitol Hill that the President-elect was positively committed to "reflation" and the abandonment of gold, and next day this news percolated to the press. On January 30 the morning newspapers of the nation carried a Washington dispatch from one of the principal press associations stating flatly that "President-elect Roosevelt has assured advisers he will sign a measure for controlled currency reflation." [2]

Senator Elmer Thomas, of Oklahoma, whose printing-press-money measures already were before the Senate Banking and Currency Committee, read this dispatch into the *Congressional Record* on January 30. Although it was the subject of editorial comment in every section of the country, the report never was repudiated by Mr. Roosevelt or anyone authorized to speak for him.

---

[2] Fraser Edwards, Universal Service, Washington Herald, January 30, 1933, as printed in the *Congressional Record*, January 30, p. 2957.

While the President-elect was represented as being open minded on the proper plans to adopt [this Washington dispatch ran], he was said to be prepared to accept some form of currency inflation in order to raise commodity prices and ease the financial stringency of the nation. He is still studying the question.

As a consequence of this commitment, Senator Carter Glass, Democrat, of Virginia, according to his friends, is hesitating about accepting the post of Secretary of the Treasury, which, they say, has been offered to him by Roosevelt. . . . This issue has been dinned into the ears of Roosevelt by both Democratic and Progressive partisans. They say they have his promise to accept some plan worked out by the new Democratic Congress.

It was such direct warnings of inflation which, from day to day, extended the old fears of the banking community to an ever enlarging circle of the general population. Simultaneously, men recognized as being high in the councils of the Democratic party converted large sums into gold, or purchased substantial interests in gold mines at home and abroad. As these operations were bruited about, new banking pressures developed in many localities. And now, because of the recently extended monthly publication of R.F.C. loans, these new pressures fell upon an emergency credit agency of government which had been greatly weakened as a dike against the gathering psychosis of fear.

Slowly at first, but with steadily increasing virulence, symptoms of general panic began to appear in scattered local crises throughout the country. During January banking runs developed in San Francisco, Baltimore, St. Louis, Kansas City, New Orleans, Cleveland, and Boston. Again and again, through the intervention of President Hoover and the R.F.C., these menacing situations were caught by the prompt mobilization of private and governmental credits. Often these White House banking conferences extended far into the morning hours. Repeatedly during this period of increasing stress, however, Mr. Roosevelt declined to quiet mounting public alarms by a reassuring word on money. As those who discussed the issue with him whispered his evasions in the market places the prairie fire of panic spread to a national inferno.

The recrudescence of acute panic psychology in January and February 1933 is exhibited in striking form in the following tabulation of R. F. C. loans to credit institutions. Observe that the monthly volume of loans swelled steadily from February through June 1932, and then subsided consistently until December. But

by February 1933 new credits were demanded again at the panic
levels of April and May in the previous year.

## TABLE III

| Month | R.F.C. loans to credit institutions |
|---|---|
| February, 1932 | $ 45,000,000 |
| March | 127,000,000 |
| April | 188,000,000 |
| May | 236,000,000 |
| June | 331,000,000 |
| July | 123,000,000 |
| August | 105,000,000 |
| September | 41,000,000 |
| October | 31,000,000 |
| November | 32,000,000 |
| December | 65,000,000 |
| January, 1933 | 64,000,000 |
| February | 178,000,000 |

The same story is told in the record of bank failures. The
next tabulation, compiled from daily reports by the Comptroller
of the Currency, indicates the net balance of deposits frozen in
bank suspensions each month, after deducting deposits released
by banking resumptions:

## TABLE IV

### Bank Failures

| Month | Balance of Deposits |
|---|---|
| September, 1931 | — $229,247,000 |
| October | — 466,284,000 |
| November | — 54,898,000 |
| December | — 258,472,000 |
| January, 1932 | — 207,915,000 |
| February *(R.F.C. began operations)* | — 42,536,000 |
| March | + 4,142,000 |
| April | — 20,572,000 |
| May | — 1,156,000 |
| June *(R.F.C. publicity campaign began in Congress)* | — 121,160,000 |
| July | + 21,216,000 |
| August | + 3,985,000 |
| September *(Maine election Sept. 12)* | + 574,000 |
| October | + 18,402,000 |
| November *(Election Nov. 8)* | — 30,832,000 |
| December | — 63,580,000 |
| January 1933 | — 120,547,000 |

*(+ equals resumed; — equals suspended)*

Nor can there be any question as to the geographical origin

of the panic pressures which precipitated the national crisis in January and February 1933. They did not come from abroad, as had the gold pressures of the autumn of 1931 and the spring of 1932. The gold position of the United States improved steadily from June 1932 to January 1933. In December 1931 our total gold holdings were $4,460,000,000, of which $459,000,000 was in foreign earmark. But in December 1932 our monetary gold stock was $4,505,000,000, with only $71,487,000 held for foreign account. Despite this increase of $432,513,000 in net gold holdings, however, metallic hoarding began at home early in January 1933, and throughout February steadily expanding hoarding and export exerted ever enlarging drain on bank reserves. The following excerpt from the annual review of *The Wall Street Journal*, summarizing American gold movements during 1932, emphasizes that, owing to the withdrawal of stocks earmarked for foreign account, the position of the dollar at the beginning of January 1933 was more secure than at any time since September 1931:

When the Bank of France completed its earmarking operations in the middle of June [1932], the panic ceased overnight. Foreign balances had been cut to a minimum and with a favorable balance of international payments the dollar began to improve in the exchange market immediately. Gold has been pouring into the country for the last half year, until monetary gold stocks now amount to $4,505,000,000, completely wiping out the losses of earlier 1932. Today [January 3, 1933] the position of the American dollar is the strongest of years, because the gold which is now coming into the country has not been accompanied by a corresponding increase in foreign short term balances. The gold which is being received truly belongs to this country as a result of its position as a creditor nation, and there can be no strings attached to the metal as formerly.[3]

If, as the record shows, our domestic banking disasters of 1931 and early 1932 flowed directly from the pressures of the international gold panic, how explain the acute revival of these same banking stresses in January 1933, after the gold battle had been won so decisively?

But while the growing fears of the nation concerning money were controlling at the beginning of 1933, they were by no means the only factors undermining national confidence. During January and early February fears of the New Deal accumulated from many directions.

---

[3] For details on American gold movements in this period see Table I, p. 5.

First, reflation or inflation obviously entailed abandonment of gold payments; and this, in turn, forewarned of repudiation of the gold obligations of the United States government. With this thrust at the federal credit, all other credit instantly wobbled. Banking operations became a mere race for complete liquidity. Gold hoarding was intensified, and every weekly report of the Federal Reserve Board during January offered unmistakable evidence of the steadily expanding flight of capital.

Secondly, in the face of heavy inroads upon our export trade by depreciated-currency countries, the spokesmen of the New Deal continued to dwell upon the wisdom of prompt *downward* revision of American tariffs. The daily discussion of Mr. Roosevelt's campaign pledge to reciprocal tariff treaties was another cloud of uncertainty over all American industry.

A bill to rectify automatically prevailing American tariffs by the degree of currency depreciation in the exporting country was pocketed by the House Ways and Means Committee throughout the entire month of January. Finally forced to the floor, it was rejected by the House on February 15, the day after the Michigan bank suspension.

Third, the retroactive publication of the R.F.C. loans on January 25 had excited needless fears for the safety of banks in some 2,000 communities.

Fourth, the overthrow of the budget-balancing tax and economy program in the House gave promise of a continued expansion of governmental spending, as another certain drive toward inflation.

Fifth, the incessant public discussion on Capitol Hill of "revolution" and "dictatorship" against the summer's background of farm strikes, hunger marches, bonus expeditions, and other mob demonstrations, stirred many excitable minds to genuine fears for the very security of government.

On February 9, for example, Speaker Garner issued through the press a statement to the effect that a dictatorship appeared to offer the only solution of national difficulties.

On February 13, Mr. Bernard M. Baruch expressed the opinion before Senator Harrison's special "Recovery Committee" that he viewed the situation of the country as "the most serious in history." Declaring that "inflation is the path to ruin," he warned that "the mere talk of inflation is retarding business." To his mind, he added, "devaluation would be disastrous."

Because of their close association with the New Deal, Messrs. Garner and Baruch now were widely credited with accurate fore-knowledge of Mr. Roosevelt's projected policies. Their statements, therefore, commanded the excited attention of the press.

By millions of men and women, all these doubts and misgivings were translated quickly into protective and defensive actions. In a word, the nation began to dig in—against a gathering storm which even those who soon were to grip the wheel of national destiny could not appraise save in hysterical forebodings of dictatorship.

Nor was the end yet. During January there emerged the further threat of the wildest economic fantasies in the now in-escapable special session of the Seventy-third Congress. On January 21 Mr. Roosevelt had outlined at Florence, Alabama, his plan for the Tennessee Valley Authority, which contemplated not only a fabulous expenditure of federal funds, but a direct plunge into government ownership of power utilities.

The domestic allotment plan of farm relief, written by Profes-sors Tugwell and Wilson, and sponsored before the House Agri-cultural Committee by Henry Morgenthau, Jr., had passed the House on January 12 and was now before the Senate committee. The ultimate cost of this venture, not even its authors dared esti-mate. In no small degree, this measure contemplated the national-ization of agriculture.

Meanwhile, the "Brain Trust" had assumed a role of increasing importance in the Warm Springs conferences, and some of its fore-most members now were having visions in public. There was large talk of a grandiose plan for the enforced consolidation of the railroads under a transportation "czar." In newspaper discussions, estimates of the proposed public works scheme ran as high as $10,000,000,000! On January 24, Senator Burton K. Wheeler, of Montana, forced a Senate vote on his resolution to authorize the free and unlimited coinage of silver at the ratio of 16 to 1. The proposal was tabled, but it commanded no less than 35 affirmative votes. Next day from Mr. Garner's office came the "retroactive file" on R. F. C. loans.

Throughout January and early February the convergence of all these fears, alarms, and uncertainties completely undermined business confidence. All new enterprise was suspended. Unemployment continued to increase. Under these aggravations, the general attitude of caution and groping in business and banking, was whipped at length to a nation-wide frenzy of flight. In both commodities and securities prices turned to a downward trend.

The whole course of this slow disintegration, after a period of substantial recovery, is clearly traced in the following tabulation of the Dow-Jones average prices for 30 leading industrial shares on the New York Stock Exchange:

TABLE V

| Date | Closing 30 Industrials |
|---|---|
| July 8, 1932 *(depression low)* | $40.56 |
| August 8 | 67.71 |
| September 7 | 79.93 |
| September 13 *(Maine election Sept. 12)* | 69.85 |
| October 8 | 61.17 |
| November 9 | 61.67 |
| December 8 | 60.05 |
| January 3, 1933 | 59.29 |
| February 3 | 58.11 |
| February 14 *(Michigan bank holiday)* | 56.57 |
| February 21 | 53.99 |
| February 26 | 50.16 |

In this table we find a statistical summary of the entire period July 1932–March 1933. Six months of incessant political hacking at recovery finally accomplished its great work. By February 1, 1933, recovery sentiment of the nation had been completely shattered. Confidence was in flight—credit paralyzed.

This same movement of recession after recovery is traced in Table VI, the Department of Labor's weighted food index.[4]

As all these mutually aggravating fears spread from day to day, the nation fell into a veritable frenzy of bewilderment and dismay. In the last week of January hoarding of currency was resumed on a steadily increasing scale, accompanied this time by a notable abnormal demand for gold. Anticipating huge profits from the now clearly indicated dollar revalorization, shrewd finan-

---

[4] United States Department of Labor, *Retail Prices*, April, 1933. 1913 = 100. Figures for the 15th of each month.

Table VI

| Month | Food Index |
|---|---|
| June 1932 | 100.1 |
| July | 101.0 |
| August | 100.8 |
| September | 100.3 |
| October | 100.4 |
| November | 99.4 |
| December | 98.7 |
| January 1933 | 94.9 |
| February | 90.9 |
| March | 90.5 |
| April | 90.4 |

ciers who were accurately informed of Mr. Roosevelt's day-to-day conversations at Warm Springs began to export gold balances. In refuge against the anticipated repudiation of the gold clause, many speculators and investors dumped government bonds upon the market in wholesale lots for gold—thus further increasing the panic pressures upon the investment portfolio of every bank. Trade advices in Wall Street—which were privately confirmed in official Washington—told of large gold operations by men close to the President-elect.

At about mid-January, Mr. James H. Rand, another recognized adviser of Mr. Roosevelt on monetary policy, had taken the lead in exploiting "The Committee For the Nation to Rebuild Prices and Purchasing Power." This group at once flooded the press with inflation propaganda. And as this new enterprise took hold nationally late in January word circulated freely in the Capitol that Mr. Roosevelt had assured Mr. Rand of full support for dollar revalorization as soon as the Committee's work adequately had prepared the ground of public opinion. These reports were strongly supported by the announcement on January 21 that Professor George F. Warren, now a foremost figure in the Brain Trust, had been appointed economic adviser to the Committee For the Nation. Mr. Henry A. Wallace, who already was under discussion as prospective Secretary of Agriculture, was a member of Mr. Rand's Executive Committee. It was known also in New York and Washington during late January and early February that at least one influential sponsor of the Committee For the Nation had exported gold balances to Canada. Other financial operators, marked for their intimate contacts at Warm Springs, were widely credited by the most reputable sources with large speculative purchases of silver.

All these anticipatory actions by men known to enjoy the confidence of the President-elect or his intimate advisers, left a far-reaching train of violent repercussions in the financial markets. In every important banking center apprehensive "blue chip" depositors began to withdraw their balances, many now insisting upon gold payments.  The withdrawal of bank balances in currency indicates fears for individual banks; but withdrawals of gold indicate something far more disturbing—fears for the stability of the government's monetary policies.  Thus, there has not been so much as one day of free gold movement in the United States since Mr. Roosevelt's inauguration, on March 4, 1933.

The resultant steady withdrawals of gold in the larger cities enforced the calling of bank loans to the interior.  This, in turn, compelled a further tremendous liquidation of bank credit.  The consequent intensification of the bankers' rush for liquidity served only to aggravate the credit pressures in two directions—first, by further crippling production and distribution in virtually every field, and secondly by feeding the fears of even the calmest depositors for the safety of their banks.

As commercial funds thus were withdrawn from rural banks, the full force of all the panic focused first upon the smaller depositories in the country districts.  With each new wave of R.F.C. "publicity runs" country banks toppled in all sections of the country.  From the outlying centers, the general panic spread slowly to the intermediate towns, and then to the larger cities.  This process first reached its inevitable climax in Michigan, on February 14.

The Michigan bank holiday proclamation was a signal to the entire nation that, with soft money now clearly in prospect, panic was upon the land.

CHART IX

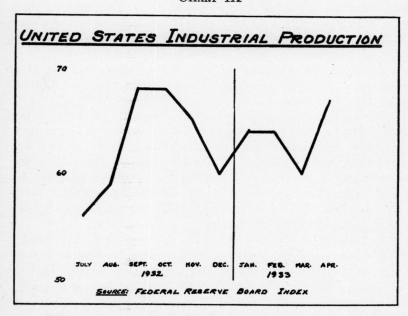

UNITED STATES INDUSTRIAL PRODUCTION

70

60

50

JULY  AUG.  SEPT.  OCT.  NOV.  DEC.  JAN.  FEB.  MAR.  APR.
1932                              1933

SOURCE: FEDERAL RESERVE BOARD INDEX

*Recovery advanced sharply with the world tide between July and September, 1932. The movement lost stride with the Maine elections in September, and then fell off alarmingly after the national elections early in November. From December, the chart movements reflected the confused approach of the banking crisis, as detailed in the next chapter.*

CHART X

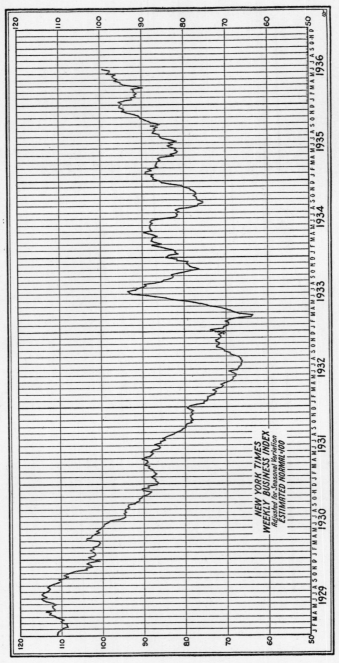

NEW YORK TIMES
WEEKLY BUSINESS INDEX
Adjusted for Seasonal Variation
ESTIMATED NORMAL=100

*Every reputable economic authority tells the same story of the sharp business upturn in the summer of 1932. "The New York Times" Weekly Business Index, generally recognized as one of the most scientifically weighted in the United States, illustrates our post-election nose-dive with admirable clarity. The above graph also is of rare value for the character of the general economic movement in the United States during the two years following the inauguration of President Roosevelt, on March 4, 1933. Such violent conflicting movements on a composite chart were unknown previously in modern economics.*

# Chapter VII

## MICHIGAN GOES UNDER

THERE had been a statewide banking moratorium in Nevada late in October, 1932, but because the difficulties there were principally of purely local origin and character the bobble did not excite any considerable general alarm beyond San Francisco. The first signs of abnormal national strains began to appear in December. Successively there occurred runs on country banks and loan associations in Arkansas, Illinois, Iowa, Minnesota, Missouri, Tennessee, Pennsylvania, Washington, and Wisconsin; and in these widely scattered local crises there appeared the first symptoms of crumbling public confidence.

From the country banks in December, the landslide of local panics spread to several secondary cities. In January, incipient runs developed in Little Rock, Chattanooga, Mobile, Memphis, St. Louis, and Cleveland. Early February brought similar developments in New Orleans, San Francisco, Kansas City, Nashville, and Baltimore. That each of these outbreaks was quieted by effective emergency action in Washington is testified by the fact that none attracted nationwide attention at the time. In only two cases did there occur even a complete city-wide banking suspension for so much as one day. Throughout this period President Hoover still was convinced that, by checking local fires as they developed, the national lines might be held against general disintegration until Mr. Roosevelt should determine his course. On February 3, however, the President-elect sailed from Jacksonville, Florida, for a two-weeks vacation aboard Mr. Vincent Astor's yacht *Nourmahal*.

As each new local banking crisis resulted in generally tightened national pressures, every community tended more and more to draw into itself. By early February the quick mobilization of reserves, the transfer of adequate protective funds from city to city, and the prompt enlistment of emergency currency from industry to tide local banks over their runs, had become practically impossible. During the first week of February warnings of a money panic began to appear in the daily reports of the Comptroller of the Currency.

The first manifestation of panic, of course, is an insensate demand for currency. Here is what happened in this direction in

February, as reflected in the Federal Reserve Board's reports of average *daily* increase in currency circulation:

| Week Ended | Average Daily Increase |
|---|---|
| February 1 | $ 5,800,000 |
| February 8 | 7,600,000 |
| February 15 | 20,100,000 |
| February 22 | 19,100,000 |

To gauge the violence of these demands one need but recall, that at the height of the international panic which followed England's abandonment of gold, in September, 1931, American currency expansion never exceeded the rate of $100,000,000 a week. But for the two weeks February 9-22, 1933, additional currency was demanded at the average rate of $118,000,000 a week. And this, as it turned out, was only the beginning of the storm. Below are the Federal Reserve Board's daily figures for the last ten days of the crisis:

| Date | Currency Increase |
|---|---|
| February 23 | $ 38,000,000 |
| February 24 | 51,000,000 |
| February 25 | 65,000,000 |
| February 27 | 187,000,000 |
| February 28 | 207,000,000 |
| March 1 | 174,000,000 |
| March 2 | 241,000,000 |
| March 3 | 454,000,000 |

During the entire year 1932 currency circulation had fluctuated around the base of $5.6 *billions*. But in the single month of February 1933, there was a net increase of $900,000,000, and of this increase, roundly $140,000,000 was in gold and gold certificates. From $6,545,000,000 on February 28, the Federal Reserve circulation leaped to a high of $7,538,000,000 for the week ended March 8, the first week of the national suspension.

In Detroit the pressures of this general panic, which began to be felt late in January, focused upon a local banking situation already greatly weakened by the extreme severity of the depression in that region. The automobile makers had been hit harder than any other major industry, and Detroit was, in a broad sense, a "one-industry" metropolis, almost entirely dependent upon the automobile. Unemployment on a scale unparalleled in any other great industrial city had piled up a staggering volume of delinquent municipal taxes; and in the face of greatly reduced revenues the city faced a relief burden which had increased steadily during three years. With municipal bonds in default, city finances were almost entirely upon the shoulders of local bankers and industrialists, as became clear in Detroit's municipal fiscal reorganization in 1933. Upon all these extraordinary local stresses and strains now fell the weight of the gathering national money panic.

On Thursday, February 9, officers of the R.F.C. were informed that Detroit was in a precarious situation. President Hoover immediately took the lead in the battle to hold that salient.

The R.F.C. examination showed that Michigan banking was dominated by two important Detroit groups. The First National group, which had deposits of $420,000,000, carried a considerable volume of slow real estate loans. While this group were in a position to pull through on their own account, obviously they could not withstand the shock of a failure in the other important group. Up to this point the First National had made no application for R.F.C. assistance.

The Guardian Trust group, which comprised some twenty banks with combined deposits of $260,000,000, had borrowed $15,000,000 from the R.F.C. in July-September 1932, and now applied for $50,000,000 more.

As a beginning, the Guardian group proposed to segregate some $90,000,000 in slow mortgage assets in a new corporation, pledging the entire assets of this liquidating company for the R.F.C. loans of $65,000,000. At the moment the market value of these assets was put at approximately $35,000,000, although the ultimate liquidation value was estimated at between $75,000,000 and $85,000,-000, depending upon the vigor of national recovery. The R.F.C. directors ruled that under the circumstances they could not extend so large a loan, more particularly because Senator Couzens, of Michigan, had threatened to carry the whole case to the Senate floor if any loan were extended save upon security approved by himself. Here the first Michigan rescue plan collapsed.

Upon further analysis of the situation, it appeared that the weakest member of the Guardian group was the Union Guardian bank. Against deposits of $20,000,000 it held not more than

$6,000,000 in "present value" assets, although it was earning approximately $1,000,000 a year in its trust business. The other banks in the Guardian group were in fair condition and could be supported individually by the R.F.C.—if the Union Guardian could be saved.

President Charles A. Miller of the R.F.C. informed the first White House conference on February 9 that it was the unanimous opinion of all concerned that the closing of the Union Guardian would precipitate a panic which might close every bank in Detroit, even engulf the entire state of Michigan. As undoubtedly such disaster would spread to adjoining states and thereby throw possibly unmanageable burdens upon the Federal Reserve system, the Union Guardian at once became the focal point of the second rescue plan.

A further hasty appraisal of the Union Guardian position disclosed that $8,500,000 of deposits would be voluntarily subordinated, $7,500,000 by Henry Ford alone. There were $6,000,000 of good assets. Only $5,500,000 more was needed therefore to enable this weakest link to pay off the smaller depositors 100 cents on the dollar over night. All other banks in the Guardian group then could be handled individually by R.F.C. credits, which probably would aggregate $35,000,000. Thus, regarded as purely a local proposition, a matter of between $5,000,000 and $6,000,000 in emergency capital was the key to saving Detroit.

At 6 o'clock Thursday evening, February 9, President Hoover, with this picture before him, conferred at the White House with Senators Couzens and Vandenberg, of Michigan, Secretary Mills, and President Miller of the R.F.C. Senator Couzens vigorously expressed the view that the Federal Government should not support such a situation as had come to light in the Union Guardian. He was informed that the suspension of this unit under the circumstances of the moment, undoubtedly would involve more than a million depositors in the First National and Guardian groups. The Senator refused to have any part in rescuing the situation, and again warned the R.F.C. directors against leniency in the appraisal of Union Guardian assets for the purpose of facilitating emergency loans. Senator Vandenberg expressed pointed disagreement with Senator Couzens and pledged himself to assist in the Michigan rescue effort in every way possible.

Secretary of Commerce Roy D. Chapin and Assistant Secretary of the Treasury Arthur A. Ballantine were sent to Detroit late that night to bring the principals together, in an effort to work out the Union Guardian situation. This being Thursday night, it was believed by all that if the bank could be held open until Saturday noon a solid solution might be found during the weekend, Monday, the 13th, being a legal holiday. Thus, four days were at hand in which to raise $5,500,000 in new capital, to be secured by a lien against the earnings of the trust business.

Next morning, Friday, February 10, the R.F.C. directors formally approved this second plan of attack, subject to the execution of new capital subscriptions in Detroit—or the subordination of some additional deposits. During the day, Alfred P. Sloan, Jr., and Walter Chrysler were invited by telephone to be at the White House for breakfast on Saturday.

Surveying the Michigan situation next morning with President Hoover, Secretary Mills, and Mr. Miller of the R.F.C., Messrs. Sloan and Chrysler disclosed great concern, and pledged every effort in cooperation with the Washington plans. They agreed that suspension of the Union Guardian likely would precipitate general panic in Detroit. Each undertook to telephone his Detroit headquarters to direct immediate contact with Secretary Ballantine. As a further emergency aid, President Hoover ordered an examination to determine whether the R.F.C. might take over additional direct relief in Detroit, thereby to assist municipal finances and hasten a resumption of pay to school teachers, policemen, and firemen. The conference ended with a firm understanding between all parties as to this line of attack.

Late Saturday afternoon, however, Secretary Mills reported money sentiment in Detroit so bad that Mr. Ballantine was having little success in his efforts to secure new capital or the subordination of additional deposits. General fears of gold abandonment had driven all capital to the storm cellar. The normal forces of resistance which repeatedly had been mobilized effectively against such situations in other cities now were in complete disintegration in Detroit.

Early Sunday morning (February 12) Mr. Wilson W. Mills, president of the First National Bank of Detroit, telephoned the

White House to appeal for immediate R.F.C. assistance to the Detroit situation in general. He was emphatic that suspension of the Union Guardian would engulf every bank in Detroit. If the Union Guardian suspended the First National would need $200,000,000 R.F.C. cash immediately, he explained.

At 7:30 P.M. Sunday Secretary Mills reported that the day's work in Detroit had secured the adherence of less than $900,000 deposits in the subordination plan, over and above Henry Ford's balances. Nevertheless, the Detroit mobilization effort was continued until early Monday morning (a legal holiday).

At 9:30 A. M. Monday, Chairman Pomerene of the R.F.C. was called to the White House. President Hoover informed him that the national temper on gold and currency left Detroit utterly impotent to cope with its own situation. Therefore, and regardless of Senator Couzens, the R.F.C. should be ready not later than 9 P.M. Monday to announce a plan to sustain the Guardian group. Secretary Mills and Senator Pomerene agreed this was an inescapable course. At worst, it involved not more than $5,500,000 in emergency loans, and that to be protected by a lien upon the trust earnings of the Union Guardian.

Late Monday afternoon President Hoover left Washington for New York, to deliver his Lincoln Day address that evening. About 10 P.M. he telephoned Secretary Mills from New York. He learned that no additional resources could be mobilized in Detroit; that the principal industrialists of the city felt unable to subscribe emergency capital. Secretary Mills also had been informed that the Detroit bankers, now in alarmed confusion, had called Governor William A. Comstock into consultation.

A few hours later all the R.F.C. plans were brought to an end by the sudden determination of the governor to proclaim a ten-day banking holiday throughout the entire State!

This proclamation, released early Tuesday morning, February 14, was issued without consultation between Governor Comstock and the R.F.C., Treasury, or White House. By this single stroke all the ground was instantly cut from under the Washington rescue plans.

Next morning, news of the Michigan proclamation, blazoned in headlines from coast to coast, released new currents of shock and panic upon every bank in the country.

CHAPTER VIII

## ON THE BRINK

O N ANY day prior to Governor Comstock's hysterical holiday
proclamation of February 14th, $5,500,000 in emergency
capital would have enabled Detroit bankers to hold their situation.
Because of the general pressures of hoarding which flowed from Mr.
Roosevelt's monetary discussions, plus political obstructions against
the essential R.F.C. supporting credits, this capital could not
be raised. But during the five days following the State holiday
proclamation the Federal Reserve System poured $50,000,000 cash
into Detroit, and it went like water on a red hot stove.

As anticipated, the Michigan suspension at once threw tremendous pressures upon the Federal Reserve banks at Cleveland
and Chicago, as well as upon all the larger member banks in Ohio,
Indiana, and Illinois. In Washington it became apparent immediately that the nation tottered precariously on the brink of disaster. In the now enlarged plan of defense the objective became, not
to buttress a single weak spot in Detroit against local pressures, but
to protect every bank in the country against runs by frightened
depositors.

As this herculean effort was being organized in Washington the
attempted assassination of the President-elect at Miami, Florida,
on the night of February 15, sent another shock of terror through
the country. By aggravating general public excitement, this incident at once tightened all the pressures of hoarding and flight which
lay at the roots of the Michigan difficulties. Even in times of
normal economic stability any shock of civil excitement tends to
induce extreme caution in depositors and investors, and hence in
banking and finance generally. In times of great stress, the temporary effect of such excitements always is multiplied out of all
reason. Such was the effect of the attempt of the mad Zangara
upon the life of the President-elect 40 hours after the Michigan
holiday proclamation.

Obviously, the first necessity in the enlarging crisis was to
resume banking in Michigan. So long as that rash festered new
communities would be infected in an ever widening circle. But

far more important, in the national view, was the necessity of
immediate reassurance to the entire country against gold revalorization and inflation—to check the poisons of fear and apprehension
which had momentarily congealed at Detroit.  Michigan could not
be rescued apart from the national situation; but neither could
the national position be stabilized while Michigan remained closed.

At a White House conference which began at 9:30 A.M.
February 14, President Hoover surveyed the whole situation with
Secretary Mills, Governor Eugene Meyer of the Federal Reserve
Board, and Governor George L. Harrison of the New York Federal
Reserve Bank.  He proposed a clearing-house scrip plan for Michigan, under the direction of the Federal Reserve banks, each member
bank to make available to its depositors immediately in scrip the
full amount of its good assets.  Any bank deficient in assets would
be compelled at once to face its depositors with a prorata distribution of scrip.  Such a plan might be put in operation in 48 hours.
It would keep local business moving and tend to check instantly
excessive currency and gold withdrawals for hoarding.  It would,
in short, apply a tourniquet to Michigan's panic bleeding.  Thereby
it would remove Detroit immediately as a focal point of excited
attention, thus contributing immeasurably to the atmosphere essential to orderly national recuperation.

Governors Meyer and Harrison vigorously opposed the clearing-
house scrip plan, principally on the ground that it would reflect upon
the adequacy and flexibility of the Federal Reserve System.  They
urged a plan, already under consideration in New York, whereby all
banks in a given State would close one afternoon and re-open next
morning with a prorata credit to each depositor representing his
share of the bank's net assets.[1]

First, this measure would need to be passed by the Michigan legislature.  Then a complementary act authorizing national banks to
conform to the State pattern would need to be approved in Congress.
Public notice of the plan, in the legislative and Congressional discussions, likely would precipitate at once an intensified run on all

---

[1] "The banking holiday, for instance, was a totally unnecessary and out-
rageous blot on the history of the country, and if it was due to anything it
was due to the mismanagement of the Federal Reserve System." Dr. H. Parker
Willis, professor of Banking at Columbia University, in a speech at Baltimore, Md., before the American Institute of Banking, February 21, 1935.

banks, for the mere suggestion of such a plan would inform large depositors that immediate withdrawals offered complete insurance against any prorata distribution. More important, in the longer view, was the consideration that such a plan summarily applied as of a given date inevitably contemplated the wiping out of many sound banks only temporarily submerged by the extraordinary currency and gold drains of January and February. At best, the New York Plan could not be applied in Michigan for ten days. President Hoover urged the scrip plan for the interval. Governor Meyer resisted it with great vigor.

At 6 P. M. February 14, Senator Joseph T. Robinson, of Arkansas, the Democratic floor leader, informed the President he doubted whether the New York Plan legislation could be got through the Congress without exciting the entire country to an immediate general panic.

At this meeting President Hoover broached the question of a reassuring joint statement by himself and Mr. Roosevelt on the issues of sound money, a balanced budget, and world stabilization. In response, Senator Robinson expressed doubt concerning the prospect of such action on the part of the President-elect.

Next day, Wednesday, February 15, Secretary Mills discussed the New York Plan (often described in the press as the Broderick Plan) with Senators Glass and Hull. Senator Glass emphatically expressed the opinion there was no possibility of the essential Federal legislation in the remaining thirteen business days of the short session. Secretary Mills then proposed a simple joint resolution which would authorize the Comptroller of the Currency, in his discretion, to adopt in regard to national banks, in a given State, whatever State laws might be enacted for the emergency. This would clear the way for the Broderick Plan in Michigan, if the legislature later should approve it.

Senator Vandenberg undertook to steer this emergency resolution through the Senate, and Secretary Mills enlisted Speaker Garner's pledge to its prompt passage in the House. Although this agreement was reached on February 15, the joint resolution was not enacted until February 25, when it was sent to President Hoover as "the Couzens Bill." During these ten days, the pressures of national disaster had rolled steadily onward to riptide.

At 5 P. M. Wednesday (February 15), Cleveland bankers called the Treasury, Federal Reserve Board, White House, and R.F.C. to report they had been under great strain all day. They were doubtful if they could pull through until Saturday.

During the day, however, there had been another Treasury conference on the clearing-house scrip plan. Mr. George W. Davison, chairman of the New York Clearing House, who had handled the New York scrip operations in 1907, was invited to survey the proposal with Secretary Mills, Assistant Secretary Ballantine, Governor Harrison, and Henry M. Robinson, of Los Angeles, who had been acting since August as Chairman of the National Banking and Industrial Conference's Committee on Credit Policies. At this meeting it was determined that the scrip plan should be introduced immediately in Detroit. All forms and contracts already had been drawn. A complete draft of the plan had been placed in the hands of the Finance Committee of the United States Chamber of Commerce, in Washington, which was receiving many calls from all sections of the country on ways and means of checking local banking pressures. The forms and contracts also had been shipped by air mail to Detroit. Next day the scrip forms were forwarded also to Cleveland.

During the morning of February 16 a director of the Guardian group in Detroit telephoned the Treasury frantically to inquire what had become of the scrip plan. He reported that New York creditor banks had informed the directors of the First National and Guardian groups that morning that a new bank was to be established by a merger. The directors were given until 3 P. M. to accept the merger plan.

Testifying before the State inquiry into the bank holiday, on September 7, 1933, James T. McMillan, who had been a director of the First National Bank since 1919, declared it was this meeting of the First National directors on February 16, which developed "the first intimation that any of us had that there was any question about our re-opening our banks. . . . . ." [2]

The project to merge the two dominant Detroit groups under new capital control by New York was, of course, instantly rejected by the dominant Detroit interests.

---

[2] *Detroit Free-Press*, Sept. 8, 1933, page 8.

Thus, the failure of the Federal Reserve Board to apply the scrip plan, as agreed upon at the Treasury conference of February 15, had resulted in the collapse of the fifth rescue plan for Detroit. As of Friday, February 17, therefore, the Michigan situation stood exactly as it had at the close of business the previous Saturday noon, February 11.

What happened to the Detroit scrip plan between the Treasury conference on the afternoon of the 15th, and the Detroit bankers' meeting of the morning of the 16th remains one of the great mysteries of the banking crisis.

On Friday afternoon, February 17, a Democratic group, representing the House Banking and Currency Committee, called at the White House to urge a national guarantee of all bank deposits. President Hoover responded that, without assurances from the President-elect on the maintenance of the gold standard, sound currency, and a balanced budget, a bank guarantee would cost the Treasury at least $3,000,000,000. He insisted that the essential step at the moment was to stop bank withdrawals and hoarding by such assurances from the incoming Administration.

With the national situation growing more acute every hour, President Hoover, in the early hours of the next morning, addressed a letter in his own hand to Mr. Roosevelt at New York, urging him to issue a reassuring statement outlining the major policies of his Administration, particularly with reference to gold, currency, banking, and the budget. This letter was delivered to Mr. Roosevelt by a Secret Service operative from Washington on the evening of February 18, soon after the arrival of the President-elect from Miami. The text follows:

My dear Mr. President-elect:

A most critical situation has arisen in the country of which I feel it is my duty to advise you confidentially. I am therefore taking this course of writing you myself and sending it to you through the Secret Service for your hand direct, as obviously its misplacement would only feed the fire and increase the dangers.

The major difficulty is the state of the public mind, for there is a steadily degenerating confidence in the future which has reached the height of general alarm. I am convinced that a very early statement by you upon two or three policies of your Administration would serve greatly to restore confidence and cause a resumption of the march of recovery.

The large part which fear and apprehension play in the situation can well be demonstrated by repeated experience in the past few years; and the tremendous lift which has come at times by the removal of fear can be easily demonstrated.

One of the major underlying elements in the broad problem of recovery is the re-expansion of credit so critically and abruptly deflated by the shocks from Europe during the last half of 1931. The visible results were public fear, hoarding, bank failures, withdrawal of gold, flight of capital, falling prices, increased unemployment, etc. Early in 1932 we created the agencies which have steadily expanded available credit ever since that time and continue to expand it today. But confidence must run parallel with expanding credit and the instances where confidence has been injured run precisely with the lagging or halting of recovery. There are, of course, other factors but I am only illustrating certain high lights.

Within the last twelve months we have had two profound examples of the effect of restoration of confidence. Immediately after the passage of the measures for credit expansion early in 1932, there was a prompt response in public confidence with expression in rising prices, employment, decrease in bank failures, hoarding, etc., even before the actual agencies were in action. This continued until it was interrupted by the aggregate of actions starting in the House of Representatives last spring, again spreading fear and practical panic across the country. This interruption brought back all the disastrous phenomena that I have mentioned, but near the end of the session, when it became clear to the country that the revenue bill would be passed, that inflation of the currency and bonus were defeated, that the government credit would be maintained, that the gold standard would be held, etc., promptly for a second time confidence returned and ran parallel with the expansion and reconstruction measures. The country resumed the march of recovery. At once there was a rise in farm, commodity and security prices, production, industry and employment. There was a practical cessation of bank failures and hoarding, and gold returned from abroad.

This continued during the summer and fall when again there began another era of interruptions to public confidence which have finally culminated in the present state of alarm and it has transformed an upward movement into a distinct downward movement.

The facts about this last interruption are simple and they are pertinent to the action needed. With the election there came the natural and inevitable hesitation all along the economic line, pending the demonstration of the policies of the new administration. But a number of very discouraging things have happened on top of this natural hesitation. The breakdown in balancing the budget by the House of Representatives; the proposals for inflation of the currency and the widespread discussion of it; the publication of the R.F.C. loans and the bank runs, hoarding and bank failures from this cause; increase in unemployment due to imports from depreciated currency countries; failure of the Congress to enact banking, bankruptcy and other vital legislation; unwillingness of the Congress to face reduction in expenditures; proposals to abrogate constitutional responsibility by the Congress, with all the chatter about dictatorship, and other discouraging effects upon the public mind. They have now culminated to a state of alarm which is rapidly reaching the dimensions of a crisis. Hoarding has risen to a new high level; the bank structure is weakened, as witness Detroit and increased failures in other localities. There are evidences of flight of capital and foreign withdrawals of gold. In other words, we are confronted with precisely the same phenomena we experienced late in 1931 and again in the spring of 1932. The whole has its final expression in the increase of unemployment, suffering and general alarm.

During all this time the means of credit expansion have been available, but neither borrowers nor lenders are willing to act in the situation of business. While the financial agencies of the government can do much to stem the tide and to localize fires, and while there are institutions and situations that must be liquidated, these things can only be successfully attained in an atmosphere of general confidence. Otherwise the fire will spread.

I therefore return to my suggestion at the beginning as to the desirability of clarifying the public mind on certain essentials which will give renewed confidence. It is obvious that as you will shortly be in a position to make whatever policies you wish effective, you are the only one who can give these assurances. Both the nature of the cause of public alarm, and experience, give such an action the prospect of success in turning the tide. I do not refer to action on all the causes of alarm, but it would steady the country greatly if there could be prompt assurance that there will be no tampering or inflation of the currency; that the budget will be unquestionably balanced, even if further taxation is necessary; that the government credit will be maintained by refusal to exhaust it in the issue of securities. The course you have adopted in inquiring into the problems of world stabilization are already known and helpful. It would be of further help if the leaders could be advised to cease publication of R.F.C. business.

I am taking the liberty of addressing you both because of my anxiety over the situation and my confidence, from four years of experience, that such tides as are now running can be moderated and the processes of regeneration, which are always running, can be released.

Incidentally, I will welcome the announcement of the new Secretary of the Treasury, as that would enable us to direct activities to one point of action and communication with your good self.

I wish again to express my satisfaction at your escape and to wish you good health.

Yours sincerely,
(Signed) Herbert Hoover.

While President Hoover and his aids thus were trying every tack on the spreading national paralysis, Senator Clarence C. Dill, of Washington, a spokesman for the Democratic silver bloc, delivered a radio address from the capital Saturday night, February 18, over a nation-wide radio chain. "The Enlarged Use of Silver and Inflation," was his theme.

"Before I talk about using silver to stop the panic," he began, "I want to tell you why the remedies already tried have failed to end the hard times."

On the whole, the speech was merely a rearrangement of scores delivered by the silverites to empty seats in the Senate during the previous two years, but in his introductory remarks over the radio, Senator Dill used the word "panic" four times in the first 200 words.

" . . . during the first two years of the panic."

"If the people would believe the panic was to last only ninety days . . ."

"The most pitiful fact that this panic has demonstrated . . ."

Such sentiments over a national hookup were not, of course, precisely what the country needed at the moment. They helped turn jitters into convulsions.

On Sunday, February 19, the R.F.C. directors worked with Detroit all day on the telephone. They now were attempting to establish a new bank with government loans plus additional local capital. At this point only three days remained for action, for under the terms of the original Comstock proclamation, the state holiday was to end automatically at midnight on Washington's birthday, February 22. On some basis, banking must be resumed on the morning of Thursday, February 23.

On Monday, the 20th, the Treasury was informed from New York that the President-elect had called Professors Moley and Tugwell into conference on the national banking situation.

On the same day, official Washington heard of the sensational testimony of Mr. Melville A. Traylor, one of the dominant bankers in Chicago, before an executive session of the Senate Finance Committee. He had told the committee in the strongest language that a firm statement from the President-elect against inflation was the only thing which might avert a general national panic. When distraught members of the Senate committee reported this testimony to the White House (it had not yet been published in the committee hearings) they were informed confidentially of President Hoover's letter to Mr. Roosevelt on February 18. It was assumed, of course, from hour to hour, that some reply would be received.

On the morning of February 21, officials of the Chicago Federal Reserve Bank called the Federal Reserve Board in Washington to report a precarious situation in that city. Unless mounting public alarms could be quieted, this telephone report ran, the Chicago banks could not hold on until the end of the week.

And precisely at this point another staggering blow fell against monetary confidence. The morning papers of February 21 carried the news of Senator Carter Glass' refusal of the Treasury portfolio in the Roosevelt Cabinet. The profound significance of this decision was accurately projected in a New York dispatch prominently displayed in the *Baltimore Sun*:

As a matter of fact, terrific last-minute pressure seems to have been brought to bear upon Mr. Glass to take the place, some of this pressure proceeding directly from the President-elect himself, and it is freely believed in quarters very close to both men that if satisfactory assurances had been given the Senator that the new Administration under no circumstances would accept inflation as a policy, his answer would have been different.

On the other side of the picture—the Roosevelt side—we cannot at this stage absolutely close the doors of his Administration on any possible proposal that might lead to inflation. One or more such measures may be found to have merit and entitled to trial, as he sees it. For that reason, he refuses to bind himself to any rigid line of action, even though it cost him Mr. Glass' services.

Cabinet discussions in Washington at this point also disclosed that Mr. Owen D. Young, strongly recommended by many Democrats for Secretary of State, had been definitely rejected by Mr. Roosevelt because of threats from the self-styled Progressive bloc in the Senate that such an appointment could not be confirmed. It was this situation which prompted Mr. Young publicly to withdraw his name from all consideration in the Cabinet making. Here, then, were more straws in the political winds pointing sharply to soft money.

That afternoon, February 21, the Federal Advisory Council, comprising bankers from each of the twelve Reserve Districts, met at the Treasury and adopted the following resolution:

The Federal Reserve Advisory Council expresses the view that there is considerable unrest in the country, due to the uncertainty as to what the policy of the incoming Administration is in respect (1) to the necessity of balancing the federal budget, largely by reduction in expenditures; (2) the dangers inherent in the various proposals to inflate the currency, and (3) the desirability of preventing the undue expenditure of federal credit, which, if continued, will be a menace to the credit of the Government.

In view of the situation, the Federal Advisory Council believes that the President-elect should issue a statement of his policy in reference to the above problems as promptly as possible.

A member of the Council was selected to deliver the resolution to the President-elect. Again, Mr. Roosevelt declined to accept public responsibility before the hour of his inauguration on March 4.

Early in the afternoon of the 21st, Cleveland bankers telephoned the Federal Reserve Board that they were under renewed pressure, greater than during the previous week. These new pressures were attributed to the fact that New York and Chicago banks were calling loans on the midland centers, and also that large industrial concerns were transferring heavy balances from various midland cities to New York. These renewed pressures were general, and they aggravated greatly the difficulties in Michigan. Important New York loans to Detroit banks which, in all previous rescue plans, had been counted as still standing, now were suddenly called. One such loan was for $20,000,000. In all previous local runs, the major-city banks had participated vigorously in the defense operations, by making heavy advances against collateral of their correspondents. But with the publication of Senator Glass' decision and the whispered word of the President-elect's refusal to answer the Federal Advisory Council, the immediate threat of currency tinkering instantly sent all such banking support to deep cover.

Simultaneously, the spread of panic conditions to the eastern seaboard states was signalized, on the 21st, by an emergency law passed in New Jersey authorizing state banks to limit withdrawals.

During the night of the 22nd (a legal holiday) the Cleveland bankers formally requested Governor White to declare a statewide banking holiday. He declined, on the ground that such a proclamation would do more harm in the south and central sections of Ohio than good in the north. Cleveland was saved for a few days longer by a decision of the R.F.C. to make available loans up to 75 per cent of any bank's quick assets.

Meanwhile, with the unexpected news of the collapse of the scrip plan in Detroit, President Hoover had urged the R.F.C. board, on the morning of the 20th, to seek a new solution for Michigan through creation of a temporary union bank in Detroit, the R.F.C. to loan $135,000,000 on the good assets of the First National and Guardian groups. This would enable the principal

Detroit bankers to resume at once with a credit of approximately 50 per cent to each depositor's account.

Senator Couzens objected to this plan, on the ground that it favored the city banks of Michigan as against the country banks, many of which could not now resume with a 50 per cent credit. He insisted that not more than $75,000,000 should be loaned to the Detroit banks, threatening again to carry the question to the Senate floor if his views did not prevail in the deliberations of the R.F.C. board.

Here, then, the seventh Michigan rescue plan collapsed. As a result, the expiration of the State holiday proclamation on February 23 found Michigan still unprepared to resume. The official extension of the holiday proclamation, publicized throughout the nation in the morning papers of the 23rd, was still another terrific blow to banking confidence. The Michigan banks had been closed since Saturday, February 11—and yet could not resume. Many State officials learned during this period that closing banks was simple, but opening them again was quite another matter!

At about this point a third effort was made to secure joint action between the outgoing and incoming administrations. The selection of Mr. William H. Woodin to be Secretary of the Treasury having been announced on the 21st, Secretary Mills took advantage of the legal holiday on Washington's Birthday to journey to New York for a conference. Some $695,000,000 in government maturities were to be handled on March 15, and under the customary Treasury procedure, the terms of the new financing would to be announced on Sunday, March 5. Inevitably, therefore, the details of this operation would be a joint responsibility of the old and new administrations. Secretary Mills also carried to New York a detailed outline of the national banking situation. He was under instructions from President Hoover to again solicit a joint statement on money and budget, to allay the spreading national panic.

Because of many pressing engagements, Mr. Woodin could give Secretary Mills but one hour on Wednesday evening, the 22nd, and another hour on Thursday morning. On each occasion Mr. Woodin insisted the new Administration would take no action, accept no responsibility, until March 4. Secretary Mills returned to Washington on the night train Thursday.

Early in the morning of February 24th, he reported the New York situation to President Hoover.

Meanwhile, Indiana had moved toward a state banking holiday on February 23, and Arkansas on February 24. During the banking hours of the 24th, terrific new pressures developed in Baltimore. The Maryland holiday proclamation, the second state-wide suspension in ten days, came in the early morning hours of Saturday, February 25th.

That afternoon, the "Couzens Bill," permitting national banks to conform to state holiday proclamations, reached the White House and was signed promptly by President Hoover. A short and simple joint resolution designed to cope with an overwhelming national emergency, it had been ten days on the Congressional ways! There still was no reply to President Hoover's personal letter to February 18 to Mr. Roosevelt.

About the hour that President Hoover signed "the Couzens Bill," Mr. James H. Rand, Jr., chairman of the Committee For the Nation, was lunching with Professor Rexford Guy Tugwell, in New York. At this luncheon, Mr. Rand was informed by Professor Tugwell that the national banking situation undoubtedly would collapse in a few days. The responsibility would be entirely with President Hoover.

"We should worry about anything but rehabilitating the country after March 4," Mr. Rand later quoted Mr. Tugwell. The professor then outlined the plan to be put in operation after March 4. As revealed by Mr. Rand at the time (February 25), this plan contemplated (1) a gold embargo, (2) suspension of specie payments, (3) reflation, and (4) a conference of 60 industrial and banking leaders to meet with Secretary Woodin at the Treasury on Tuesday March 7 to outline an industrial rehabilitation program.[3]

Word of this plan reached the financial district in New York Saturday afternoon, February 25, but no hint of it reached the Sunday press.

With this positive assurance that gold abandonment was contemplated by Mr. Roosevelt, the financial community now began to brace itself for the final shock. It was this authoritative "inside

[3] Theodore G. Joslin, *Hoover Off the Record*, p. 364.

information" concerning the plans of the incoming administration
which controlled events during the final week of the Hoover administration.

When there is uncertainty as to the value of currency no bank is
sound.

And by February 25, 1933, the banking community had been informed four times that Mr. Roosevelt contemplated some form of
currency manipulation; first in the November-January debt conversations, when he declined to advance firm preparations for the
World Economic Conference; second, on February 21, when Senator Glass declined the Treasury portfolio; third, on February 22,
when the President-elect refused to answer the memorial of the Federal Advisory Council, and fourth, on February 25, by Mr. Rand's
disclosure of Professor Tugwell's airy "We should worry."

Side by side with the news of the Maryland collapse in the
morning papers of Saturday, February 25, was the word from Hyde
Park that "President-elect Roosevelt will not present his program
for economic recovery in his inaugural address, except in the most
general terms, it was learned today, but will reserve it for his message to the special session of Congress which he will call soon after
his inauguration.[4]

Illuminating, perhaps, as evidence of the bold courage with
which Mr. Roosevelt stepped into the Presidency is the following
report of his extended conference on Friday, February 24, with Mr.
James A. Farley, Chairman of the Democratic National Committee:[5]

Mr. Roosevelt and Mr. Farley discussed the New York state patronage
situation late this afternoon and decided on procedure to coordinate the
distribution of state and federal patronage, a system which will be put into
effect in other states.

With Democratic governors in forty-one states, Mr. Farley believes
that there should be cooperation between the national and state party
organizations in parcelling out the jobs.

He is in a position to do this effectively in New York state, because
he is both national and state chairman. For example, if a man from
Cayuga county should receive a federal post, it is Mr. Farley's idea that a
state post of equal calibre should go to a resident of some other county
than Cayuga, or at least should lessen the chance of a Cayuga resident for

---

[4] James A. Haggerty, in the *New York Times*, February 25th, 1933.
[5] *New York Times*, February 25, 1933.

appointment. He will attempt to have the various state chairmen co-operate with him, that the organization recommendations in the distribution of minor patronage will be so arranged that it will receive the widest possible distribution, thus to build up an effective party organization throughout the country. . . .

On February 26 Ohio and Indiana cities moved to protect bank depositors in various ways. On February 27, Pennsylvania, New Jersey, and Indiana authorized banks to restrict withdrawals. Next day Delaware followed.

CHAPTER IX

## THE STORM GATHERS

O N SATURDAY evening, February 25, a business associate telephoned Secretary of Commerce Chapin, himself a citizen of Detroit, that if the Michigan banks did not resume on Monday morning there would be serious rioting. All currency had disappeared.
People were unable to buy milk and bread. There was no money for
gasolene. Automobiles were locked in garages, many even stalled in
the streets. Cars of perishable foods rotted on the freight sidings.
Upward of 100,000 persons on municipal relief had been cut off without supplies for three days. The principal banks of the entire State
had been closed since February 11.

Later that evening Mr. Roy Howard, chairman of the Scripps-
Howard newspapers and a militant supporter of Mr. Roosevelt in
the presidential campaign, telephoned the White House. Just returned from Cleveland and Detroit, he expressed alarms over the
threat of civil disturbances in those cities. He sought President
Hoover's assent to his soliciting President-elect Roosevelt for some
effective joint action to check the national panic. President Hoover
explained that, with Secretary Mills, he had been endeavoring daily
since February 18 to enlist Mr. Roosevelt's cooperation in this direction. President Hoover's letter to Mr. Roosevelt under date of February 18 still was unanswered.

At 5 P. M. President Hoover conferred with Secretary Mills and
Mr. Miller, of the R.F.C., concerning the new resumption plan for
Detroit now working under R.F.C. direction. Mr. Miller disclosed
that Senator Couzens at this point was assuming the rôle of final
judge of all plans involving federal credits. He had indicated again
to the R.F.C. board earlier in the afternoon that no advance should
be made in Detroit save upon security approved by himself.

Although the directors realized fully there was no legal authority
for such interference, they were reluctant to ignore Senator Couzens
to the degree which the situation appeared to demand. On at least
two prior occasions the Senator had threatened to carry his opposition to the floor of the Senate. In the hope of avoiding the further
public excitement which this course promised, the R.F.C. directors
sought to placate the Senator at every turn, even when his demands

101

appeared wholly unreasonable, or when his discussions clearly indicated only a feeble and hazy grasp of the whole situation.

Informed from two quarters of the threats of civil disorders, Secretary Chapin pleaded with Senator Couzens Saturday night for
active cooperation in the R.F.C. rescue efforts. He warned that
further delay in Detroit might entail the gravest consequences for
the nation.

At the 5 o'clock White House conference Saturday, President
Hoover suggested that, in view of Senator Couzens' objections to the
50 per cent payoff plan, as then formulated in the R.F.C., attention
should be directed to a 25 per cent payoff. This would reduce the
contemplated R.F.C. loans to Detroit from $135,000,000 to $75,-
000,000, as demanded by the Senator.[1]

Accordingly, Mr. Miller left for Detroit Saturday night, to work
out details of what amounted to a 30 per cent resumption plan.

But on Sunday morning, February 26, Senator Couzens again
presented objections to the revised R.F.C. plan. He now requested
authority to go to Detroit as agent of the R.F.C. to settle the situation in his own way. When this request was communicated to the
White House, President Hoover responded it was now too late to
start on a new tack; that every effort should be made to resume
banking in Michigan next day; that Senator Couzens should be ignored for the remainder of the day. At the same time Secretary
Chapin was urged to work with Detroit by telephone all day in an
effort to secure the acceptance by all interests of the new R.F.C.
plan. This he did, and with considerable success.

By Sunday evening the R.F.C. had perfected this eighth resumption plan for Michigan. As regards Detroit, it involved a large
subscription of new capital by Mr. Henry Ford, to launch a merged
bank. It also contemplated the temporary freezing of many important deposit accounts, a large R.F.C. loan on approved assets of the
two principal banking groups, and a thirty-day "stand-still" on a
number of loans from New York banks. As these loans already

---

[1] Between March 1933 and November 1934 the R. F. C. advanced more
than $310,000,000 to Michigan banks, to hasten resumptions and liquidations.

Up to June 30, 1936, the R.F.C. authorized loans aggregating $2,563,556,000
to maintain banking operations. Of this total, $1,339,556,000 was in assistance
to operating banks, and $1,224,000,000 to receivers, conservators, or other
liquidating agents of closed banks.

were impounded by the State-wide banking suspension, their extension under the R.F.C. plan had been regarded throughout the involved negotiations as merely a matter of legal formality.

At 8 P. M. Sunday Assistant Secretary Ballantine carried from the Treasury to the White House the tentative drafts of the Detroit resumption announcements. All was in readiness.

At 9 P. M. the Cleveland Federal Reserve Bank telephoned that, with the new R.F.C. aid, Cleveland would be able to resume Monday morning, on a limited withdrawal basis. At last the clouds appeared to part. Cleveland would be saved and Detroit resumed.

Suddenly, like a bolt of lightning, word flashed from Detroit that the New York banks involved would not support the new plan with extensions of their present loans.

Crash! went the eighth rescue plan for Detroit.

So there was no resumption in Michigan that Monday.

Meanwhile, since Saturday afternoon, word of Professor Tugwell's plans for dealing with the crisis had penetrated to the remotest corners of the banking world.

Clearly, it was a gold suspension.

Inauguration now was but five days forward.

CHAPTER X

RIPTIDE!

FROM midnight Sunday, February 26, the battle in Washington became one to hold and check a certain nation-wide panic.
During Monday gold withdrawals mounted hourly. Reserve city
banks pulled their funds from the secondary centers. From coast
to coast panicky depositors converged on their banks. Michigan
ceased to be the first line of defense.

A measure of the times is given in the fact that serious street
rioting in Detroit Saturday, Monday, and Tuesday hardly was
noted in the national press. At this point every city in the
country had its own grave problems in banking. Detroit's misery,
manifest in disturbances which ordinarily would have dominated
every front page in the United States, was wholly submerged.

Only Washington now could maintain instant touch with the
swiftly developing crises on a hundred fronts. There, the whole
panorama was visible from hour to hour. The Federal Reserve
Board, in constant leased-wire communication with the twelve
Reserve cities, was informed early Tuesday morning, February
28, that Chicago banks could not weather another day such as
Monday had been. Cleveland already was on a limited withdrawal
basis. Indiana officials were discussing a state holiday proclamation. As the riptide of disaster swept over new cities, beleaguered
bankers turned frantically to Washington, some demanding cash
by airplane!

On Monday morning, February 27, Secretary Mills conferred
again with Mr. Woodin, this time in Washington. On this occasion Mr. Woodin communicated frankly once more that he was
under firm instructions from the President-elect to take no part
in any joint action between the outgoing and incoming administrations. He acknowledged that Mr. Roosevelt's policy would be to
take over the situation at the lowest point possible.

This policy had been hinted in Professor Tugwell's "We-should-
worry" statement to Mr. Rand on February 25, which had been
communicated to the White House during the same afternoon,[1]

---

[1] Joslin, *op cit.*, p. 364.

and also in the failure of the President-elect to reply to President Hoover's letter of February 18. Mr. Woodin's polite but obviously painful aloofness in all the banking conferences, both in New York and Washington, now confirmed this policy again.

Thus, it was recognized clearly in official Washington during the last week of the crisis that, while only vigorous joint action to check gold withdrawals and currency hoarding could save the nation from a complete banking paralysis, Mr. Roosevelt had no intention of joining President Hoover in any such action. Mr. Roosevelt, it will be recalled, had intimated twice in his war-debt communications to the White House in November that he would assume no responsibility until March 4. And this policy, save in covert relation to budget and farm legislation, since had been confirmed in every public act of both the President-elect and all his recognized spokesmen and advisers.

Nor could President Hoover appeal to public opinion. To have revealed starkly to the nation the critical situation now in flow would have been to precipitate instantly the very collapse the White House still was bending every effort to avert.

Monday, February 27, passed with still no reply from Mr. Roosevelt relative to the President's proposals of February 18.

A quick glance backward to then current business and economic surveys presents vividly the situation in which the country floundered during this last week of February. Said a leading New York bank in its regular monthly review:[2]

Such developments seem to have been due, at least in part, to the publication of the names of borrowers from the R.F.C. The latter institution was formed for the purpose of aiding banks and other business organizations that possessed inherently sound assets, in the hope that such support would not only help them to meet current demands, but also inspire confidence in their soundness and, to that extent, make actual financial aid unnecessary. The publication of the names of borrowers seems to have gone far toward nullifying the psychological benefits that appeared to be accruing from the Corporation's activities. . . . The fear of inflation has, of course, been increased by the failure of Congress to deal in any adequate way with the financial emergency of the federal government. A seriously unbalanced government budget is always a cause of misgivings on the part of the business community, not only because it carries a threat of higher taxes and excessive public borrowings, but also because it creates a situation which, unless corrected within a

---

[2] *Guaranty Survey*, Guaranty Trust Co., New York, February 27, 1933.

reasonable time, reaches a point where it becomes virtually impossible for the government to meet its obligations without resorting to inflationary methods.

Nor were these views confined to the United States. From London came the weekend survey:[3]

> The judgment of financial circles here is that at no time in the recent economic history of America has there been greater need than at present for a flat declaration of sound monetary policy by the new American government. It is believed that if the inflation bogy is definitely laid by the new administration, the first long step toward restoring confidence will have been taken.
>
> If America were also to recognize the importance of a settlement of the international debt question, it would give marked impetus to confidence abroad and would necessarily have favorable repercussions in America.
>
> Europe has undoubtedly been disturbed by the apparently increasing American opinion in favor of currency inflation and the innumerable schemes which have been proposed to restore business and raise prices.

Under the same date, the Paris review began:[4]

> The confusion of mind on Europe's markets concerning the future tendency of the dollar must be ascribed in great measure to lack of information regarding the definite intentions of the new American government. A declaration by Mr. Roosevelt declaring firm resolution to maintain a sound currency would have an extremely reassuring effect. So would a plain statement on the economic policy which he proposes to pursue.

By a curious coincidence, these views were echoed impressively in America. On Monday, February 27, Mr. Alexander Dana Noyes, financial editor of the *New York Times,* appeared before the Finance Committee of the Senate, then conducting a special inquiry into ways and means of promoting business recovery. He ascribed the world depression to the inexorable forces of war liquidation, and vigorously urged international cooperation to maintain sound currencies and restore trade. The *Times* account of Mr. Noyes' lengthy statement continued:[5]

> Speculation so drained Europe of capital, said Mr. Noyes, that its financial foundations were taken away, and only world-wide action could now restore international trade and confidence. . . . Rehabilitation of nations in the past took place, not through rash experiments with currency, said Mr. Noyes, but by the application of sound principles and the use of sound money.
>
> Every proposed expedient of inflation which has occupied the minds

---

[3] *New York Times,* February 27, 1933.
[4] *Ibid.*
[5] *Ibid.,* February 28, 1933, p. 27.

of men in this country in recent months had been discussed during panics in the past, he said.

After the Napoleonic Wars it was suggested in England that the content of the gold sovereign be reduced, and after the Civil War depression, free silver or paper inflation was urged.

When these ideas were rejected and the gold standard retained, Great Britain became the world's money center; and after 1873 the depression ended when specie payments were resumed.

This quite unbroken record proves, in the first place, that the return of prosperity, which always came eventually after the other periods of depression had run their course, did not in any case result from inflation or depreciation of the currency.

In the second place it proves that the positive rejection of plans urged for such purposes was in due course followed by returning prosperity.

This at least suggests the question whether the seeming deepening of the depression at the present time may not be consequence as well as cause of current talk about currency experiments.

And why not? No business plans are possible while the standard of value is at stake. Of necessity, the future is wholly obscure. The disastrous experience of other well known episodes of currency inflation is bound, on all such occasions, to impress the mind of the careful business man with a sense of utter uncertainty about the future, if not despair about the present.

The printed record of this so-called "Harrison Inquiry," which was headline news during the last phases of the banking crisis, abounds in such sentiments. Said Mr. Winthrop W. Aldrich, chairman of the Chase National Bank, in his testimony of February 22:[6]

The prestige and reputation for financial integrity of the American government, of the United States Treasury, and of the Federal Reserve banks, is one of the greatest capital values in the world, and is one of the most essential features of world financial organization. Wantonly to destroy it, quite apart from the question of morality, would be an act of economic destruction of fearful magnitude.

On the previous day Dr. Nicholas Murray Butler, president of Columbia University, had said:[7]

In the case of the United States it is, in my judgment, imperative that public budgets, whether federal, state, county, or local, be immediately balanced, and that the habit of public borrowing to meet current costs of government be brought to an end. . . . There must be no tampering with the foundations of our monetary system. . . . The crux of the whole situation, however, is to be found in international understanding and international cooperation.

Thus, if, at the end of February, the country was in the last

---

[6] *New York Times*, February 23, 1933, p. 26.
[7] *New York Times*, Feb. 22, 1933, p. 8.

agonies of an utterly insane money panic there lay beneath it all
some firm ground of doubt in the minds of prudent and reputable
observers of world affairs.

On Tuesday, February 28, new State holidays were proclaimed in
Nevada, Alabama, Kentucky, and Tennessee; and two downtown
banks suspended in the District of Columbia, one of them within a
city block of the United States Treasury. In terms of deposits, each
of the Washington suspensions was far less important than any one
of hundreds which had occurred throughout the country during the
previous ten days. With reference, however, to the accumulative
impact upon national psychology, they were tremendously important. From New York to San Francisco the headlines screamed,
"Washington Bank Suspends!" In many persons for whom the last
glimmer of confidence was sustained by faith in the power and authority of the Federal government, as symbolized in the very word,
"Washington," the capital's closed banks turned quavering doubt to
dark despair. If banks could fail in the shadow of the United States
Treasury, at the very door of the R.F.C., what then?

During the morning President Hoover called Secretary Mills and
Governor Meyer, of the Federal Reserve Board, to the White House
to canvass again what had come to be known as the active deposit
guarantee plan. This plan contemplated the segregation of all bank
deposits into two categories, active and inactive. The active deposits were to be represented by immediate liquid assets of the bank,
the inactive, by deposit certificates as a lien upon slow assets over
the liquidation period. All active accounts then were to be guaran-
teed by the Federal government for one year. A heavy penalty was
prescribed for bankers who distorted asset values in prorating active
deposits.[8]

The essence of this plan was that it preserved a maximum fluid-
ity of each bank's quick assets, while yet requiring every institution
to stand on its own feet in the matter of slow assets. Later, these
slow assets could be hastened through liquidation with the aid of the
Federal Deposit Liquidation Corporation.[9]

----

[8] This, it will be noted, is the conservator plan finally adopted, in modified
form, in the Roosevelt Banking bill of Mar. 9.
[9] This agency had been recommended in President Hoover's message to
Congress, December 5, 1931.

Governor Meyer opposed the plan, principally because the percentage of active deposits credited to each account would reveal publicly the net position of every bank in the country. But since the New York Plan[10] urged by Governors Meyer and Harrison two weeks earlier, now had proved ineffective in Michigan—because the legislature would not pass the necessary enabling act—Governor Meyer assented tentatively to further study of the active deposit guarantee plan by the Federal Reserve Board. All documents necessary to the application of the plan had been prepared, and copies transmitted to the Federal Reserve Board. The conference arose with a decision to approach Mr. Woodin once more with a plea for joint action along this line.

In the face of the whirlwind now clearly gathering, President Hoover addressed a second personal appeal to Mr. Roosevelt, urging, in view of the proximity of inauguration, that the President-elect be prepared to assemble the Seventy-third Congress in extraordinary session on Monday, March 6. At the moment news reports from Hyde Park were to the effect that there appeared to Mr. Roosevelt to be no need for a special session until April. Discussing the prospective April session in a Washington dispatch to the *New York Times,* on February 27, Mr. Arthur Krock had said:[11]

. . . That would suit Mr. Roosevelt. He has told many of his visitors that he does not want to summon Congress until "all the i's are dotted and all the t's crossed" in the bills which constitute his legislative program for the extra session. This position is warmly endorsed by the Congressional leaders. . . .

During the afternoon Secretary Mills conferred with Mr. Woodin on the active deposit guarantee plan. The adoption of this plan, of course, would require immediate action in both Houses of Congress. Only Wednesday, Thursday, and Friday remained, for the inaugural ceremonies were scheduled to begin Saturday morning at 11. Obviously no such legislation could be got through Congress without the public approval and immediate political support of the President-elect. But after his conference, Secretary Mills reported Mr. Woodin as still firm in his refusal of any joint action.

Next day, Wednesday, March 1, President Hoover received a direct response from Mr. Roosevelt. This communication was at once

[10] Page 88, *et seq.*
[11] *New York Times,* February 28, 1933, p. 4.

a reply to the President's letters of February 18 and February 27. It was a pointed rejection of President Hoover's plea for joint action to restore confidence in the currency. The text of this letter follows:

February 28, 1933.

Dear Mr. President:

I am dismayed to find that the inclosed, which I wrote in New York a week ago, did not go to you, through an assumption by my secretary that it was only a draft of a letter.

Now I have yours of yesterday and can only tell you that I appreciate your fine spirit of cooperation and that I am in constant touch with the situation through Mr. Woodin, who is conferring with Ogden, and with various people in N. Y.

I am inclined to agree that a very early special session will be necessary —and by tonight or tomorrow I hope to settle on a definite time—I will let you know.

You doubtless know of the proposal to give authority to the Treasury to deposit funds directly in any bank.

I get to Washington late tomorrow night and will look forward to seeing you on Friday.

Sincerely yours,
(Signed) FRANKLIN D. ROOSEVELT.

The President,
The White House.

(Enclosure)[12]

Dear Mr. President:

I am equally concerned with you in regard to the gravity of the present banking situation—but my thought is that it is so very deep-seated that the fire is bound to spread in spite of anything that is done by way of mere statements. The real trouble is that on present values very few financial institutions anywhere in the country are actually able to pay off their deposits in full, and the knowledge of this fact is widely held. Bankers with the narrower viewpoint have urged me to make a general statement, but even they seriously doubt if it would have a definite effect.

I had hoped to have Senator Glass' acceptance of the Treasury post— but he has definitely said no this afternoon. I am asking Mr. Woodin tomorrow. If he accepts, I propose to announce it tomorrow together with Senator Hull for the State Department. These announcements may have some effect on the banking situation, but frankly I doubt if anything short of a fairly general withdrawal of deposits can be prevented now.

In any event, Mr. Woodin, if he accepts, will get into immediate touch with Mills and the bankers.

Very sincerely yours,
(Signed) FRANKLIN D. ROOSEVELT.

The President,
The White House.

_____
[12] Undated.

Mr. Roosevelt's belated reply to President Hoover presents three questions of fundamental historical bearing:

First, how explain the misplacement of the earlier response (the enclosure of March 1) in the Roosevelt home for a whole week? By the text of the covering note of February 28, the enclosure had been penned on February 21. But at February 21 Mr. Roosevelt already foresaw that "a fairly general withdrawal of deposits" could not be prevented "now." No one else viewed the situation in that light as early as February 21. Only Michigan then was under a holiday proclamation. Maryland's State-wide suspension, the second in the list, still was four days forward.

The record shows that the situation here seen by Mr. Roosevelt on February 21 did not actually develop until Monday, February 27, or the day before the letter was transmitted to Washington. The question arises fairly, therefore, whether this enclosure actually was penned in final form "a week ago," or some time later, when the developing crisis made some answer to Hoover inescapable. At least, this theory appears more credible than the explanation offered—that a communication upon matters of such grave import, addressed to the President of the United States, had been filed inadvertently.

Secondly, the general situation in banking (as of February 21) was by no means so hopeless as Mr. Roosevelt appeared at the moment to believe; for within four weeks of that date banks carrying 93 per cent of all deposits had been found, upon Federal audit, eligible to resume under Mr. Roosevelt's personal certification of soundness. Obviously Mr. Roosevelt did not intend to say on February 21, that slow or frozen assets representing approximately 7 to 10 per cent of all deposits must certainly carry down the entire banking structure of the United States.

The third question presented concerns Mr. Roosevelt's guiding policy in the whole situation. "The real trouble is that *on present values* very few financial institutions anywhere in the country are actually able to pay off their deposits in full . . ." Does not this statement, coupled with Senator Glass' rejection of the Treasury portfolio the same day, seal the evidence that the President-elect already had determined upon reflation, inflation, or revalorization— to change these troublesome "present values"? [13]

---

[13] This policy already had been announced in the press of January 30 (page 70).

And if inflation had been determined upon, might it not have been of some assistance to the President of the United States to know the stark truth promptly in confidence? At least the Hoover defense measures might then have been suited to the real situation, rather than to one half concealed by Mr. Roosevelt's adroit political maneuvers.

This decision of the President-elect was in hand for the morning conference at the White House March 1. With President Hoover were Secretary Mills, Assistant Secretary Ballantine and Governor Meyer. The President asked if there were any other measures which still might be successful in Congress. None could be suggested. The President insisted that, with inauguration only three days forward, no sweeping executive action now could be effective without Mr. Roosevelt's public support. He suggested, therefore, a new beginning by the Federal Reserve Board on the clearing-house scrip plan. As two weeks before, Governor Meyer offered vigorous opposition. He also repeated his opposition to the active deposit guarantee.

The President then urged that the active deposit guarantee plan be offered in Congress with Mr. Roosevelt's legislative support. It was agreed to sound Mr. Woodin again on this proposal. That evening Secretary Mills conferred with Mr. Woodin in New York. Mr. Woodin reported that Mr. Roosevelt would accept no responsibility until noon March 4.

As ten States now had declared various types of bank holiday, it was obvious, as Mr. Roosevelt acknowledged in his first letter to the President, that Washington no longer could hope to stem the panic with merely a reassuring joint statement on gold, currency, and budget. Efforts now must be directed, first to applying an effective tourniquet to the bleeding banking structure; then to measures of rehabilitation.

Thus had the crisis mounted from week to week. On February 14 the problem had been to resume Detroit promptly and assure the nation on currency. Eight specific Hoover proposals on this situation had been defeated or obstructed. By February 25 the problem had become one of checking an incipient nation-wide money panic. But until March 1 Mr. Roosevelt did not even reply to President Hoover's personal plea for a reassuring joint statement on gold, money, and budget policies.

Now, by March 1, the problem had become one of bracing the nation against a complete suspension of banking.

# CHAPTER XI

## CRASH!

**A**FTER dinner, President Hoover conferred with Assistant Secretary Ballantine on a proposal to go before Congress next day, Thursday, March 2, with the active deposit guarantee plan. From the White House Mr. Ballantine talked over the telephone with Messrs. Woodin, Meyer, Harrison, and Moley, in New York. Mr. Woodin repeated to the New York conference that he had positive instructions not to support any joint action. He also declined an expression on the national plan for clearing house scrip.

Next morning, March 2, Secretary Mills was able to report to the White House at 9:30 A.M. that the principal New York banks had braced themselves for a heavy blow, but that all believed themselves in shape to escape suspension.

After this report on the conclusions on the New York meeting of Wednesday evening, President Hoover repeated to his Thursday morning conference advisers, including Secretary Mills, Assistant Secretary Ballantine, and Henry M. Robinson, that another effort to enlist Mr. Roosevelt's cooperation in an emergency legislative program now had proved unavailing. For the rest, the overnight news was only that holidays had been proclaimed, or were in preparation in Arizona, California, Louisiana, Mississippi, Oklahoma, Oregon, and Nebraska.

Later Thursday morning, Secretary of the Interior Ray Lyman Wilbur called at the Executive Offices. During an informal chat he offered the sentiment that everything humanly possible had been done to avert disaster; but now the battle was over; inauguration was but forty-eight hours ahead; in view of the situation in Congress and the attitude of the President-elect, there appeared little probability that any effective action could be accomplished in the interval.

While the Secretary spoke, he related afterward, the President looked sternly into his face. Almost before Wilbur had concluded his sentence, President Hoover answered explosively; "We will fight until 10:49 A. M. March fourth, when I leave for the Capitol! We must try everything, not once but a dozen times!"

After luncheon, Senators Robinson and Glass were called to the White House. Senator Glass explained that final action on the Glass Banking Bill, which included the general deposit liquidation plan to be administered with government capital, was held up by differences between Speaker Garner and Chairman Steagall, of the House Banking and Currency Committee. At President Hoover's behest, Senator Glass said he would urge Mr. Roosevelt to intervene in favor of this bill. The President then gave the two senators a complete picture of the national situation, concluding that as so many states now were on holiday vigorous federal action obviously was imperative. He outlined four possible plans of action: (1) a scheme of Treasury deposits, as then being formulated by Mr. S. Parker Gilbert in conferences with Mr. Roosevelt's New York advisers,[1] (2) a temporary government guarantee of all deposits, (3) the Broderick, or New York Plan, which had been rejected by the state legislatures, or (4) the active deposit guarantee. He insisted that the Democrats in Congress must pledge advance support of any plan offered formally. If none of these plans could be supported, the President added, he would support any plan Senator Glass could approve. The discussion revealed that Mr. Roosevelt had not up to this point considered any specific plan for national action *prior* to March 4, and that plans to be launched by the new Administration after that date still were in a very nebulous state. In conclusion, Senators Robinson and Glass agreed that, under the circumstances, nothing could be accomplished in the remainder of the Congressional session—that, with only Friday and Saturday morning remaining, it would be futile to attempt effective legislation. They agreed, however, to transmit the President's proposals to Mr. Roosevelt. Concerning this offer of joint action, no answer ever came to the White House.

At about 6:30 P.M. Thursday, March 2, Mr. Adolph Miller, a member of the Federal Reserve Board who had conferred with Mr. Roosevelt at Albany since the election, called at the White House. During the course of a long talk, he suggested the possibility of a one-week banking moratorium under the authority of the Enemy Trading Act. This step had been outlined in the tenta-

---

[1] This plan had been mentioned sketchily in Mr. Roosevelt's letter of February 28.

tive program held in readiness at the Treasury for several weeks in June and July, 1932, when the foreign metallic raids had carried America to the brink of gold suspension.

Attorney General Mitchell held this authority for a national bank suspension to be tenuous, but agreed the step might be ventured if Mr. Roosevelt would proclaim his support and approval. However, unless the President-elect would undertake to bring the House Democrats into line instantly, no such step could be considered. A Presidential holiday proclamation affecting 50,000,000 depositors could not be risked if it were to be challenged by angry partisanship in Congress.

Even at this point, President Hoover held that a complete banking suspension was wholly unnecessary if hoarding were checked; nevertheless he remained willing to accept suspension if Mr. Roosevelt held that to be the only solution of the crisis. Failing, however, to enlist Mr. Roosevelt in any proposal for legislative action, the President turned once more to the possibility of a joint proclamation forbidding gold withdrawals, currency hoarding and gold export. This, he held, would check panic withdrawals until Mr. Roosevelt might take over on Saturday. Mr. Miller expressed his tentative agreement; whereupon Mr. Woodin was urged to solicit Mr. Roosevelt's cooperation in this step. At the same time, Secretary Mills urged Senators Hull and Byrnes to recommend this course upon the President-elect.

Later in the evening, the Federal Reserve Board in Washington received a second suggestion for a national bank holiday, this time through the New York Federal Reserve Board. The New York Board reported Mr. Woodin had signified his assent to a joint proclamation. Thereupon, the holiday proclamation was drafted anew in Washington, after the old forms. But at 11:15 P.M. the New York Conference telephoned that Mr. Woodin was having difficulty obtaining Mr. Roosevelt's approval. Fifteen minutes later Secretary Mills advised President Hoover that Mr. Roosevelt had declined to support the proclamation.

Although visibly distressed by his chief's repudiation of his own commitments to the holiday, Mr. Woodin remained in conference with the New York bankers. Shortly after midnight Mr. Woodin urged Secretary Mills to proclaim a one-day holiday. President

Hoover responded he would issue such a proclamation if Mr. Woodin would support it under his own name.  Mr. Woodin declined, reiterating he was under instructions from his chief to take no part in any banking program before March 4.

This conversation ended the White House effort of Thursday, March 2. It was, in fact, something after 2 A. M., March 3.

At his morning conference, Friday, March 3, President Hoover again canvassed the possibility of some effective action to check currency hoarding and gold withdrawals over the week-end.  Obviously the nation now was in an utter frenzy to turn everything into cash.  Overnight, new state holiday proclamations had been announced in Georgia, Idaho, New Mexico, Texas, Utah, Washington, and Wisconsin.  Similar decrees were partially in force or in preparation in Colorado, Connecticut, Maine, Massachusetts, Pennsylvania, New Jersey, Rhode Island, South Dakota, West Virginia, and Wyoming.  The Federal Reserve Board reported gold withdrawals now at the unprecedented figure of $1,389,000,000. The governors of the New York Stock Exchange were discussing suspension of the market.

Secretary Mills telephoned Senator Byrnes to again solicit the cooperation of the President-elect in a proclamation against hoarding and gold export.  Senator Byrnes responded that Mr. Roosevelt, the night before, had been firm in his position against any action before March 4.

Early Friday morning (March 3) authoritative word passed in the New York financial community that Messrs. Leffingwell and Gilbert, of the firm of J. P. Morgan and Company, were working on a national banking plan with some of Mr. Roosevelt's advisers.  As then outlined, this plan contemplated a special "asset currency" to be circulated through the Federal Reserve Banks, against collateral deposits by both member and non-member banks. News of this project sealed the already widespread knowledge that the President-elect definitely had decided to abandon gold.  In some banking circles there still remained grave doubt whether such "asset currency" could be forced into circulation, but that weakness in the technical aspects of the scheme did not in any way detract from its significance as an indication of Mr. Roosevelt's inclinations and purposes.

It was demonstrated, of course, during the national suspension which followed the inauguration, that asset currency could not be circulated in any considerable amount so long as the nation remained technically on gold. Nevertheless, the news of this project, on March 3, again confirmed, as had every move of the President-elect since November, that Mr. Roosevelt was inclined strongly in the direction of gold abandonment and managed currency. It was the spread of these suspicions, and their repeated confirmation between November and February, which completely undermined recovery and precipitated the February-March panic. Now, on March 3, definite news of the "asset currency" plan made fact of every suspicion in this direction, and swept away instantly the last support of monetary confidence.

Up to this point calm men might have looked at the basic economic factors in our gold position and felt every confidence in the ultimate security of the dollar; now they were compelled to take note of the purely political factors which were operating quite independently of controlling economic considerations. News of Mr. Roosevelt's "asset currency" project, therefore, was the figurative last straw. It broke the confidence even of those who stubbornly held their faith in American gold and money through the last week of February.

Early in the evening of March 3 Secretary Mills was informed that events suddenly had swept to an acute crisis in New York and Chicago. During the day the larger New York banks had lost $110,000,000 in gold to foreign account, plus $20,000,000 gold to others. From New York approximately $200,000,000 had been withdrawn to the interior. New York bankers reported to Governor Harrison, at the New York Federal Reserve Bank, that they could not stand this drain another day—not even for the half day Saturday, inauguration day.

President Hoover again offered a joint proclamation with President-elect Roosevelt against excessive currency withdrawals and gold exports, or to himself promulgate any plan submitted by Mr. Roosevelt with the approval and support of Senator Glass or the Federal Reserve Board.

Mr. Roosevelt, being now in Washington, called the White House from his suite in the Hotel Mayflower about 8:30 P.M. to ask what the President thought of a national bank holiday. The President responded that a joint proclamation against excessive withdrawals of currency and gold, and controlling gold exports, should suffice for Saturday morning. A general suspension, without a definite plan for resumption to be indicated at the moment, appeared to President Hoover to be unnecessarily drastic—even dangerous. As for the control method, that proclamation long had been ready at the Treasury and could be issued within the hour if Mr. Roosevelt would signify his approval. The President-elect asked for time to discuss the matter with Governor Lehman, of New York, who then was in conference with the New York bankers and members of the Federal Reserve Board.[2]

At 9:30 P.M. Secretary Mills, Attorney General Mitchell and Henry M. Robinson entered the White House. Secretary Mills reported the New York Reserve bankers now were demanding a national holiday. President Hoover again stated that such action, without a simultaneous declaration of the resumption method and policy, would needlessly destroy deposit values throughout the length and breadth of the land. He insisted no man should close all the banks in the country until he knew how and when they might be opened again; and since the resumption plan must rest entirely in Mr. Roosevelt's jurisdiction, consultation and coopera-tion between the two administrations appeared not only essential, but inescapable if the national welfare figured as a factor in the equation. He again suggested a proclamation against excessive withdrawals of gold and currency.

During the White House conference, Governor Harrison again telephoned from New York to urge a national holiday proclama-tion. President Hoover repeated what he had just stated to his White House conference. Within the hour Governor Meyer tele-phoned from the Federal Reserve rooms in the Treasury to demand a national holiday proclamation. Governor Meyer now was empha-

[2] "Probably the most astonishing and disappointing feature of the bank crisis was the demonstrated impotence of the Federal Reserve System to retain control over the situation. For nearly twenty years Americans have believed with implicit confidence that money panics in this country were things of the past, and that we should never experience another. Neverthe-less the money panic of February and March proved to be by far the most disastrous of our entire history."—*Report of the Economic Policy Commis-sion of the American Bankers Association*, April 12, 1933, p. 6.

tic in the view that the proposed gold and hoarding control would not suffice for Saturday morning. With this view, however, Dr. Adolph Miller expressed polite disagreement.

Shortly before midnight President Hoover called Mr. Roosevelt to ask if he had reached a decision on the joint proclamation against excessive withdrawals. Mr. Roosevelt responded that Governor Lehman had been informed by his New York advisers that there would be no need for a general suspension.

Mr. Roosevelt added that he did not wish a national holiday proclaimed at this time, for he wished to study the situation and perfect his own program *after the inauguration*. He explained that Senator Glass, who had been with him at the Mayflower for an hour, concurred in the view that a national suspension was not necessary. The President-elect also said he f<sup></sup> 'ed Senator Glass' plan for bank scrip. Meanwhile, however, he declined to join or support President Hoover in a proclamation to control gold withdrawals. This conversation offered the first direct intimation to the White House that the President-elect still was wholly without a positive and definite plan of action to be followed from noon next day.

President Hoover asked the President-elect to hold the telephone while these views were repeated to his White House conference. In a voice that also carried through the telephone to the Mayflower, Mr. Roosevelt's sentiments, as above, then were repeated to the four men surrounding the President's desk. The conversation ended with the understanding that Mr. Roosevelt did not want, and would not support, a national bank holiday proclamation, or any other joint action with President Hoover. The hour was midnight March 3.

At about 4 A. M. (March 4) arrangements were perfected in both New York and Chicago for State holiday proclamations to govern Saturday, inauguration day.

At 10:30 P. M. on Sunday, March 5, President Roosevelt released at the White House his historic proclamation closing every bank in the land.

There was, at that moment, no known plan for the resumption.

This action climaxed the nation's forty-day drift to disaster.

A hard-won recovery now lay in tragic ruins.

"A few weeks after his inauguration Mr. Roosevelt had converted a rout into a surge of recovery. One of the means by which he accomplished the change was by letting the dollar depreciate. Since departure from the old gold standard was so evidently salutary in its effects, Mr. Roosevelt probably would like the credit for having planned it. I suspect he had it in mind all along as a possibility or perhaps as an inevitability. However, it was quite clear from his campaign utterances and from his efforts to draft Senator Glass as Secretary of the Treasury that he intended to try to avoid it."

—Ernest K. Lindley,
*Half Way With Roosevelt*
*(September, 1936; p. 97)*

# NOTES ON THE BIBLIOGRAPHY

Source material on the 1933 banking suspension in the United States is voluminous, but widely scattered. Most of the statistical material available thus far appears only as incidental matter in various appraisals of President Roosevelt's monetary policies.

In the meantime, however, sufficient material has become available to throw the major events of the crisis into tentative historical focus. For those who may be interested in a more detailed reconstruction of certain pivotal episodes than the plan of this book would permit, the principal source material and official surveys are indicated below.

American Bankers Association, several reports of the Economic Policy Committee during 1932 and 1933, especially *Banking After the Crisis,* and *The Guaranty of Bank Deposits.* Also a 1935 report on *The Bank Chartering History and Policies of the United States.* (For a condensed, authoritative chronology of banking history in the period October 1932-July 1935, see *Banking's Reference Supplement,* a special supplement to the *Journal of the American Bankers Association* for March, 1936.)

Angell, James W., *Gold, Banks, and the New Deal,* in the *Political Science Quarterly,* American Academy of Political Science, New York, Vol. XLIX, No. 4, December, 1934.

Bremer, C. D., *American Bank Failures,* Columbia University Press, New York, September, 1935 (especially tabulation of forced liquidations and consolidations after the 1933 suspension).

Federal Reserve Board, The—*Documents Relating to the National Bank Holiday,* June, 1933. Also the regular monthly *Bulletin* for April and May, 1933. Also the *Annual Report* for the calendar year 1932; same for 1933.

Hoover, Herbert, *The Challenge To Liberty,* Charles Scribner's Sons, New York, 1934 (especially those sections of Chapter VI which deal with Managed Currency, centralization of credit control, and government management of foreign exchange).

Hoover, Irwin H., *Forty-Two Years In the White House,* Houghton Mifflin Co., New York, 1934 (especially sections on November and January White House conferences between President Hoover and Governor Roosevelt).

Ickes, Harold L., *Roosevelt As I Know Him,* in the *Saturday Evening Post* for August 15, 1936 (especially the section, *Meeting the Bank Crisis*).

Joslin, Theodore G., *Hoover Off the Record,* Doubleday-Doran, New York,

1934 (especially Chapters XX and XXX, dealing with establishment of the R.F.C., and the rising tide of hoarding in February, 1933).

Lindley, Ernest K., *The Roosevelt Revolution*, The Viking Press, New York, 1933 (especially the several sections dealing with Mr. Roosevelt's shifting views on money and federal finance between the 1932 election and the inauguration).

Lindley, Ernest K., *Half Way With Roosevelt*, The Viking Press, New York, 1936 (especially Chapter IV for Mr. Roosevelt's views on the banking crisis as it developed from day to day in February, 1933).

Myers, William Starr, and Walter H. Newton, *The Hoover Administration*, Charles Scribner's Sons, New York, 1936 (especially Chapters VI to XVI, inclusive, tracing American policy from the German moratorium of 1931 to the 1933 inauguration).

Peek, George N., *In And Out*, in the *Saturday Evening Post* for May 16, and June 6, 1936 (especially valuable for documentation of confused policies of Roosevelt administration during 1933 and 1934 in relation to foreign trade as a function of money).

Reconstruction Finance Corporation, *Annual Reports*, for 1932, 1933. Superintendent of Documents, Washington, D. C.

Roosevelt, Franklin D., *On Our Way*, John Day Co., New York, 1934. Also, *Looking Forward*, 1933.

Senate Committee on Banking and Currency, Hearings, January and February, 1933, S. Res. 56, 72nd Congress and S. Res. 97, 73rd Congress, 1st session (especially that phase of the investigation popularly known as the Pecora Inquiry into the Michigan Suspension, in the U. S. Senate Library).

State of Michigan, *Hearings Before the Special Referee Inquiring Into the State Banking Holiday*. Printed as official document of Wayne County Circuit Court, Detroit, 1934.

Sullivan, Mark, *America's Official Point of View on the Debts*, in the *Saturday Evening Post*, May 13, 1933 (especially valuable for light on diplomatic relation of European war debts to world disarmament and monetary stabilization).

Upham, Cyril B., and Edwin A. Lemke, *Closed and Distressed Banks*, The Brookings Institution, Washington, D. C., November, 1934.

Vanderlip, Frank A., *Tomorrow's Money*, Reynal and Hitchcock, New York, 1934 (especially sections on banking policy in New York State under Governor Franklin D. Roosevelt).

Warburg, James P., *The Money Muddle*, Alfred A. Knopf, New York, 1934 (especially chapters dealing with United States monetary policy in the London Economic Conference of 1933, to which Mr. Warburg was one of the American delegation).

# INDEX

German reparations, 24
Gilbert, H. Parker, 114
Glass, Senator Carter, 2, 3, 20, 71, 95, 114, 117, 119
Gold—panic in 1931, 1; international run ends July, 1932, 3; movements to and from U. S., 5; Roosevelt campaign strategy on, 21, 24; revalorization proposed, 42; how 1932 panic checked, 73; position U. S. dollar at January, 1933, 73; exports by Committee For Nation, 77; withdrawals in January, 1933, 78; panic traced by Hoover, 91; revalorization intimated four times by President-elect Roosevelt, 99; withdrawals week of February 25, 104; new panic at March, 116
Goldsborough, Rep. Allen, 19, 70
Government re-organization — Hoover's 58 executive orders rejected in Congress, 62
Great Britain—asks revised war debt plan, 27; conditions future war debt installments, 36; accepts invitation of Roosevelt, 41
Green, William, President of A.F.L., 52
Guarantee of bank deposits—proposed in Congress, 91; suggested by Hoover, 108
Guaranty Trust Co., 105
Guardian Trust Co., Detroit, 83

Harrison, George L., 88, 113, 117, 118
Harrison, Senator Pat, 107
Hoarded currency, index of, 44
Home Loan Bank, organized, 14
Hoover, Herbert—recommends Glass-Steagall Act, 2; policies against depression, 14; German moratorium, 14, 24; ratified, 25; policies touching money, stabilization, tariffs and disarmament, 26; telegram to Roosevelt on war debts, 27; message to Congress, 1932, 36; on currency hoarding, 44; resists R.F.C. publicity, 48, 50, 52; reorganization orders, 62; letter to Roosevelt on panic, 91
Howard, Roy W., 101
House, Col. E. M., 39, 62

Insull, Samuel, 4

Inflation — announced as Roosevelt policy, 70; opposed before Senate Finance Committee, 94

Jones, Jesse, H., 47

Kreuger, Ivar, 4

Lausanne conference, 14, 24
Leffingwell, a Morgan partner, confers, 116
Legislative obstruction in Congress, 3
League of Nations economic survey, 6
Lehman, Governor Herbert H., 118, 119
Lindley, Ernest K., 21, 120
Lindsay, Sir Ronald, 41
Lippmann, Walter, 11
Literary Digest, quoted, 31
London view of U. S. crisis, 106

MacDonald, Ramsay, 26
Maine elections of 1932, 9
Maryland bank holiday, 98
McCain, Charles S., 52
McKellar, Sen. Kenneth D., 64
McMillan, James T., 90
Meyer, Eugene, 88, 89, 108, 109, 112, 113, 118
Michigan bank holiday, 50, 78, 81, 82, 83, 86, 87, 88, 97, 103
Miller, Adolph, 114, 115, 118
Miller, Charles A., 84, 107
Mills, Ogden L., Secretary of the Treasury, 30, 31, 60, 69, 85, 89, 90, 101, 104, 108, 109, 112, 115
Mills, Wilson W., 185
Mitchell, Wm. D., Attorney General, 115, 118
Moley, Prof. Raymond, 30, 31, 41, 68, 94, 113
Monetary stabilization, 26
Moore, Gov. A. Harry, 53
Morgan, J. P., 16

National Credit Corp., 3, 44
New Deal, fears of in Jan., '33, 74
New York Herald-Tribune, 34
New York State bank holiday, 119
New York Stock Exchange, 116
New York Times, 34
Nourmahal, 51, 81
Noyes, Alexander D., 106

Ohio bank holiday, 100

Paris views on crisis, 106
Party conventions 1932, 6
Peek, Geo. N., 22